Producer Organisations:
A Guide to Developing Collective Rural Enterprises

Oxfam GB

Oxfam GB, founded in 1942, is a development, humanitarian, and campaigning agency dedicated to finding lasting solutions to poverty and suffering around the world. Oxfam believes that every human being is entitled to a life of dignity and opportunity, and it works with others worldwide to make this become a reality.

From its base in Oxford in the United Kingdom, Oxfam GB publishes and distributes a wide range of books and other resource materials for development and relief workers, researchers and campaigners, schools and colleges, and the general public, as part of its programme of advocacy, education, and communications.

Oxfam GB is a member of Oxfam International, a confederation of 13 agencies of diverse cultures and languages, which share a commitment to working for an end to injustice and poverty – both in long-term development work and at times of crisis.

For further information about Oxfam's publishing, and online ordering, visit www.oxfam.org.uk/publications

For information about Oxfam's development, advocacy, and humanitarian relief work around the world, visit www.oxfam.org.uk

Oxfam Skills and Practice

Books in this series offer practical guidelines for development and humanitarian practitioners. Based on Oxfam's programme experience, they are designed to consolidate and share learning, and encourage good practice. Below is a list of recent titles in the series. For a full and up-to-date listing see our website: www.oxfam.org.uk/publications

Building Capacity Through Financial Management
by John Cammack, 2007

Cash-Transfer Programming in Emergencies
by Pantaleo Creti and Susanne Jaspars, 2006

Effective Consultancies in Development and Humanitarian Programmes
by John Rowley and Frances Rubin, 2006

Producer Organisations:
A Guide to Developing Collective Rural Enterprises

Chris Penrose-Buckley

Front cover (left to right)
San Fernando, Chile: Peach harvest at Patricio and Victor Vilches' farm
(Toby Adamson/Oxfam)
Artibonite, Haiti: A truck being loaded at a market, Pont-Sondé
(Toby Adamson/Oxfam)
Honduras: The Dalia's organic coffee for sale in the tourist shops of Copan Runias
(Gilvan Barreto/Oxfam)

Spine
Hajmel, Albania: A bottle of wine produced by the wine-makers' association Zadrima Malore
(Christian Guthier/Oxfam)

Back cover
Honduras: Sacks of coffee beans being stored at La Central's high-tech coffee-processing plant
(Annie Bungeroth/Oxfam)

First published by Oxfam GB in 2007

© Oxfam GB 2007

ISBN 978-085598-575-2

A catalogue record for this publication is available from the British Library.

All rights reserved. Reproduction, copy, transmission, or translation of any part of this publication may be made only under the following conditions:
- with the prior written permission of the publisher; or
- with a licence from the Copyright Licensing Agency Ltd., 90 Tottenham Court Road, London W1P 9HE, UK, or from another national licensing agency; or
- for quotation in a review of the work; or
- under the terms set out below.

This publication is copyright, but may be reproduced by any method without fee for teaching purposes, but not for resale. Formal permission is required for all such uses, but normally will be granted immediately. For copying in any other circumstances, or for re-use in other publications, or for translation or adaptation, prior written permission must be obtained from the publisher, and a fee may be payable.

Available from:

Bournemouth English Book Centre, PO Box 1496, Parkstone, Dorset, BH12 3YD, UK
tel: +44 (0)1202 712933; fax: +44 (0)1202 712930; email: oxfam@bebc.co.uk

USA: Stylus Publishing LLC, PO Box 605, Herndon, VA 20172-0605, USA
tel: +1 (0)703 661 1581; fax: +1 (0)703 661 1547; email: styluspub@aol.com

For details of local agents and representatives in other countries, consult our website: www.oxfam.org.uk/publications or contact
Oxfam Publishing, Oxfam House, John Smith Drive, Cowley, Oxford, OX4 2JY, UK
tel +44 (0) 1865 472255; fax (0) 1865 472393; email: publish@oxfam.org.uk

Our website contains a fully searchable database of all our titles, and facilities for secure on-line ordering.

Published by Oxfam GB, Oxfam House, John Smith Drive, Cowley, Oxford, OX4 2JY, UK

Printed by Information Press, Eynsham

Oxfam GB is a registered charity, no. 202 918, and is a member of Oxfam International.

Contents

List of case studies vi
About the guide vii
Introduction viii
Part I: The rationale for producer organisations
   1. Defining features of producer organisations 2
   2. Small-scale producers and the market 5
   3. The rationale for producer organisations 18
   4. Who benefits from producer organisations? 26
Part II: What do producer organisations look like and how do they operate?
   5. Producer organisation activities and services 32
   6. Producer organisation structure 37
   7. Producer organisation governance and management 46
   8. Producer organisation business strategies 53
   9. Producer organisation access to market services 64
   10. Influencing the market environment 67
   11. Producer organisation development stages 72
Part III: Working with producer organisations
   12. The role of development NGOs 79
   13. Initial steps and considerations 88
   14. Facilitating the producer organisation support process 100
   15. Supporting advanced producer organisation activities 129
   16. Forming new producer organisations 136
Endnotes 139
Annex 1: Further reading and resources 141
Annex 2: Rapid assessment of markets and producers 144
Annex 3: Producer organisation capacity appraisal 148
Annex 4: Potential implication of different legal structures 156
Annex 5: Building blocks for a strong foundation 160
Glossary 162
Bibliography 170
Index 178

List of case studies

1. Agrolempa, El Salvador 32
2. Clam Clubs, Viet Nam 38
3. National Smallholder Farmers' Association of Malawi (NASFAM), Malawi 43
4. Union of Peasants and Associations of Southern Niassa (UCASN), Mozambique 46
5. Olive-oil Co-operatives, Palestine 54
6. Zadrima Co-operative, Albania 56
7. Oorvi Agricultural Products, India 60
8. Asprepatía, Colombia 69
9. Kiwi Growers' Co-operative, Georgia 92
10. Aprainores, El Salvador 94

About the guide

This guide was produced as part of an initiative to share Oxfam GB's knowledge and experience of supporting producer organisations. This initiative was managed by Oxfam GB Programme Advisers, David Bright and Annabel Wilson. The content of the book builds on discussions between Oxfam GB programme staff and partners that took place at a workshop on producer organisations in March 2006. Case studies included in the guide were contributed by: Caroline Abu-Sada, Sally Baden, Craig Castro, Manuela Mece, Aida Pesquera, Nguyen Quang Quynh, Eliso Tkhadaia, Carlos Vargas, and Amit Vatsyayan.

The guide was edited by David Bright and Annabel Wilson.

Acknowledgements

In addition to the important contributions from Oxfam GB staff, this book draws on research findings, lessons, and insights from individuals and organisations and these sources have been acknowledged wherever possible in the text and in the bibliography. The theoretical framework on producer organisations and markets that has informed part of this guide owes much to Andrew Dorward, Jonathan Kydd, and Colin Poulter at Wye College, Imperial College London. Special thanks to Ian Barney, Alison Griffith, Eila Penrose, Amit Vatsyayan, Malcolm Fleming, Craig Castro, Emily Jones, Antonio Hill, Luqman Leckie, Lea Borkenhagen, Manuela Mece, and Joss Saunders for reading and offering useful comments on the manuscript. Finally, I am particularly indebted to my wife, Joanna Penrose-Buckley, for her patience, moral support, and detailed comments on many drafts.

Chris Penrose-Buckley
August 2007

Introduction

The context

In the past, rural development projects have often tried to improve the lives of small-scale producers by helping them to increase their production. In some cases, this approach delivered real benefits, but often the benefits were short-lived, as there was no market for the produce, or prices collapsed because of overproduction. Over the last decade, lessons from these failures and awareness of the new challenges presented by global markets have forced a rethink in rural development projects. Today, it is no longer enough to promote increased production: small-scale producers have to adopt a market-oriented approach if they want to compete in and benefit from local, regional, and global markets.

Small-scale producers face many opportunities but also huge challenges in today's markets. Market liberalisation since the 1980s has cut back the support services provided by the state, and forced producers to face the risks of often weak and volatile markets. With the withdrawal of state services and an end to guaranteed markets, most producers have had to produce and market their produce without access to reliable or affordable input, financial, or transport services. Meanwhile, the rapid globalisation of agricultural trade has forced many small-scale producers to compete with large commercial producers around the world and to meet tough quality and safety standards demanded by buyers. Furthermore, those who are able to access markets often find themselves at the mercy of buyers who can take advantage of small-scale producers' weak bargaining position.

This guide focuses on one important strategy that small-scale producers can and, in many cases, have to adopt in order to access, compete in and influence markets. This strategy is collective action among producers in the form of producer organisations (POs). POs come in many different forms, including co-operatives, farmer associations, and informal groups of producers. A more detailed definition of POs is provided in Part I of the guide but for now we will treat a PO as an organisation of producers formed to market their produce.

Of course promoting collective action among producers is not a new approach to rural development – co-operatives have played an important role in rural development in both industrialised and developing countries for well over a century.[1] Until the early 1980s, many governments promoted rural co-operatives as a central element of their rural development policy (and often as a political tool). From the early 1980s there was less and less funding for such programmes, as the state's role and funding for agriculture were cut back, and the performance of many state-led co-operative programmes was often disappointing. Since the end of the 1990s, however, promoting POs has again become a fashionable development strategy, as a growing number of governments, donors, and non-government organisations (NGOs) have recognised the need for POs to help small-scale producers compete in liberalised markets.[2] The problem is that small-scale producers, in particular women and other marginalised producers, very often lack the skills and resources to develop strong POs that can provide the services required by their members, influence policy decisions that affect their future, and compete in the market. To succeed, POs need a wide range of support services and that is what this guide is about.

The actors

There are many different actors and organisations that provide business services and other kinds of support to POs. Figure 1 identifies various organisations that have a specific interest or mandate in developing the capacity of POs (i.e. not just in doing business with POs). Government ministries and agencies, donors, development NGOs, and specialist support agencies may all provide special support to POs as a means of achieving rural development objectives, while buyers, such as exporters and alternative trading organisations, may also provide special support to POs to improve the capacity of producers to supply the products they want to buy.

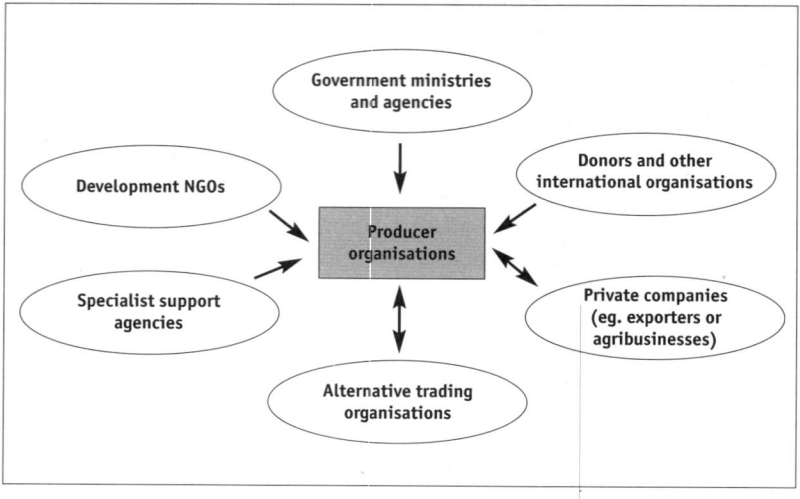

Figure 1: Actors and organisations supporting producer organisations

Purpose of this book

The purpose of this book is to provide practical guidance for the staff of development NGOs involved in supporting POs. Although Oxfam GB has been promoting and supporting POs for many years, very little of this experience has been collected and documented to help its staff and others working with POs to draw on this experience. While there are many existing guides and manuals on POs, few if any are written specifically for the staff of development NGOs. This guide therefore draws on Oxfam GB's experience of working with POs to date, as well as on a wide range of secondary research, guidance, and experience on POs.

As development NGOs often do not have the expertise and experience required to support POs effectively, especially the business-side of a PO, we do not expect their staff to get directly involved in implementing all and, in some cases, any PO support activities. Instead, this guide focuses on the role of development NGOs as donors, co-ordinators, and, especially, as facilitators of these support activities. In many cases the actual support activities, such as the training, advice, or investment, will need to be provided by specialists. However, to facilitate and co-ordinate the support process and manage the relationship with a PO effectively, staff of development NGOs will need to have a reasonable understanding of the main issues, steps, and challenges involved in the development of a strong and sustainable PO.

For most development NGOs, PO support activities will be part of a wider development programme, involving a range of development projects, which presents a challenge as well as an opportunity for their work with POs. As we argue below, small-scale producers often need additional investments and interventions in order to participate in POs, and for their POs to become sustainable businesses and organisations – so POs will often benefit from complementary development activities. However, POs can also be weakened by these activities if they undermine a PO's business. Development NGOs therefore need to integrate PO support activities carefully within their wider programmes.

This guide should help staff of development NGOs working with POs to:

- understand the main purpose and benefits of POs in today's markets;
- understand the main types, forms, and functions of POs;
- integrate PO support activities into existing development programmes;
- develop an effective partnership with a PO and other service providers;
- navigate their way through a support process, drawing on existing experience and good practice and avoiding the most common traps; and
- judge and understand when and how to bring in the expert advice and technical expertise of specialists.

Although the guide had been written with a specific audience in mind, many of the lessons and much of the guidance will be interesting and relevant to any of the actors identified in Figure 1 above, including donors, alternative trading organisations, and private companies.

A word of caution

For many people, collective action is an obvious solution to the problems faced by small-scale producers, and this view is reflected in the huge amount of recent interest in POs. However, it is important to emphasise from the very start that POs are not a universal solution to all the problems small-scale producers face.

Firstly, POs cannot fill all the gaps in the agricultural service market left by the state and which have not been filled by the private sector, after market liberalisation. POs may be able to narrow the gap and POs can make it easier and cheaper for the state and other actors to provide services to small-scale producers, but in many cases there are more fundamental constraints to market access and market development that POs alone cannot solve. While it is important for development NGOs to understand how best to operate in rural contexts where essential services are missing, it is also important not to expect too much of POs when operating in weak rural markets.

Secondly, POs tend to reflect the social context they operate in and may therefore exclude women or other marginalised groups from participating in the PO or from positions of power within the PO. Women may also be unable to participate in POs as the demands of household caring duties constrain their time and resources. POs may therefore provide limited if any benefits to poorer, marginalised producers.

Lastly, it is important to recognise that supporting POs is not always the best starting point for organisations wanting to help small-scale producers access markets. This is because there are often very basic legal, economic, or political problems preventing POs from developing successfully, and unless these problems are addressed first there is little point in investing significant resources to support POs. For example, if the laws in a country do not provide a suitable legal framework for POs to conduct their business successfully, it may be better to invest resources to help producers advocate for changes to these laws, before providing direct support to POs.

Market access and market reform

It is also important to note that this guide is not just about improving *market access* for small-scale producers. Providing support to POs can be understood as a way of levelling the playing field for small-scale producers. In other words, this support can give them a chance to compete with bigger companies and commercial farms that are able to mobilise resources and influence policies in their own favour. Although this type of support is important, it may provide few benefits if the markets POs are accessing are not functioning properly. As we will see in Part I, local and global markets are often not competitive and are often driven by the interests of buyers who are able to influence prices, impose demanding standards, and force small-scale producers to take on more and more risk. In this case, market access may not be sufficient for small-scale producers to gain real benefits from local or international trade and to trade their way out of poverty, and there is a need for additional, parallel efforts to ensure these markets become more just and competitive. The critical point is to get the right balance between market access and market reform: staff in development NGOs will often focus on unfair market structures and may not pay enough attention to the important investments needed to help producers become more efficient and competitive economic actors. Meanwhile, governments, donors, and private companies often focus on raising the efficiency of producers and helping them access markets.

They may pay insufficient attention to fundamental problems with how the market is structured and fail to recognise small-scale producers' potential role in shaping policies for market and rural development.

Language, tensions, and definitions

This is a practical guide, written for project and programme staff who have little previous experience of working with POs and supporting market-oriented development activities, and for whom English may not be the first language. It has therefore been written in simple English and, as far as possible, avoids unnecessary jargon. Where it has been necessary to use technical terms these are explained in the text or in the glossary at the end of the book.

There are some basic tensions and limitations in this guide that are worth pointing out at this stage. Although the guide is meant to be very practical and to provide step-by-step guidance, it does not provide detailed instructions on how to support every aspect of a PO's development. Not only would it be impossible to cover all this in a small book, but providing this kind of guidance would contradict the basic purpose of the guide, which is to provide a general map to help *facilitate*, not implement, PO support activities. Detailed, technical guidance on marketing, business management, quality control, and so on is provided in other manuals and is anyhow best left to experienced specialists. This guide therefore tries to strike a balance between providing practical tips and advice and offering a general overview. Annex 1 suggests further reading and help, should readers want to gain a more in-depth understanding of a particular issue.

Throughout this guide we refer to the producers we are concerned with as 'small-scale producers'. It is important to note that the term 'small-scale producer' covers a complex and diverse reality and in many countries represents a significant majority of the rural population. Small-scale producers include surplus producers who produce for the market as well as subsistence producers who often cannot produce enough to meet their basic needs and mainly engage in the market as consumers. As we will see at the end of Part I, most POs, according to the definition used in this guide, are made up of better-off but still relatively poor surplus producers, and POs often provide few direct benefits to subsistence producers, at least early on in their development.

When we refer to small-scale producers and POs in this guide we are focusing primarily on rural producers and rural POs, and therefore our attention will be primarily on agricultural producers and agricultural POs. Furthermore, much of the experience and most of the examples and case studies presented throughout the guide deal with agricultural production. Having said this, as the main focus of this guide is on facilitating PO support activities, most of the guidance will also be relevant to non-agricultural, urban-based POs, and possibly even to workers' organisations.

Structure of the guide

The guide is split into three parts. Part I outlines some of the main challenges faced by small-scale producers, explains why POs are therefore a necessary strategy to overcome these challenges, and considers some of the limitations of POs as a means of helping small-scale producers. Part II provides an overview of different types of POs and PO approaches and activities, highlighting key factors affecting PO success and important lessons based on a range of case studies and research findings. Part III then focuses on the role of development NGOs in facilitating PO support activities and provides step-by-step guidance on how to facilitate the investments and interventions required to help small-scale producers develop effective organisations and build strong collective businesses.

Part 1 | The Rationale for Producer Organisations

Orienting questions

What are the defining characteristics of POs?

What challenges and opportunities do small-scale producers face in today's global markets?

How can POs help small-scale producers to overcome these challenges?

Can POs help all small-scale producers?

1 | Defining features of producer organisations

The aim of this guide is to provide guidance for development NGOs working with many different types of producer organisation (PO), marketing different products in different countries and contexts. Our definition of POs therefore needs to be broad enough to capture these different types of PO but also narrow enough to capture the distinctive characteristics of POs that, according to this guide, make them different from other types of rural organisation, such as community-based organisations or self-help groups. We will focus on three defining features of POs in relation to their purpose, structure, and core activity. According to this guide a PO is:

- a rural *business*;
- a *producer-owned and controlled* organisation;
- engaged in *collective marketing* activities.

Producer organisations are rural businesses

According to this guide, POs are commercial organisations. To survive in the long run, POs have to provide tangible benefits to their members *and* cover their costs from their business income. This immediately sets POs apart from many other types of rural organisation promoted and supported by development NGOs: unlike village or community-based organisations, POs are not primarily a means of channelling resources to a community or of mobilising community activities. Instead, POs are businesses that aim to provide business-oriented services to their members. This does not mean that POs cannot receive financial support in the form of grants or interest-free loans. But in the long run POs need to become financially sustainable, just like any other business. This also does not mean that POs cannot pursue social objectives; in fact, a number of the POs we will encounter in this guide provide social services to their members and the wider community. For example, COMUCAP, an association of women producers in Honduras, came together to improve awareness about women's rights. The point is that for POs to succeed, the business cannot be led by social objectives even if social objectives provide the main motivation for the organisation. If social objectives are placed before business priorities, the business is likely to fail and no one will receive either economic or social benefits.

Producer organisations are producer-owned and producer-controlled

According to our definition, POs should generally be owned and controlled by their members, who are mostly small-scale producers. This means that small-scale producers should be the main owners of a PO and, conversely, that POs should not generally be controlled by external owners, who are not producers. As we will see in Part II, this definition may exclude some POs that are jointly owned by NGOs or private companies. There may be good reasons why some POs have other shareholders either during the first years of their development or even as a long-term arrangement. However, there is no harm in treating these cases as important exceptions as it reinforces the important principle that, unless there are very good reasons that are in the long-term interest of the producers, POs should be owned and controlled by their producer-members.

Producer organisations are collective marketing organisations

The third distinctive characteristic of POs is that they are collective marketing organisations. That is to say, they are organisations that collectively market their members' produce and/or that collectively supply inputs to their members. This is not a common way of defining POs, but as one of the main reasons for supporting POs is to help small-scale producers increase their competitiveness and power in markets, it makes sense to focus on organisations that actually engage with the market. Most POs carry out many other collective activities, such as collective production, processing, and influencing policy makers, but the core activity that all POs have in common is that they collectively market their members' produce.

In some ways, these defining features represent a goal rather than a fixed definition. For example, it may take many years before all the members of a PO actively participate in decision-making and therefore effectively control the organisation. The point is that a PO should be moving towards these features even if it takes many years to get there.

> **Summary: defining features of producer organisations**
>
> - This guide defines POs as rural businesses that are generally owned and controlled by small-scale producers and engage in collective marketing activities.
> - According to our definition POs can engage in social activities and pursue social objectives but these should not drive business decisions; the PO's business should be the first priority.

2 | Small-scale producers and the market

Small-scale producers face many different challenges and opportunities in today's markets. This chapter provides an overview of some of the main changes in national, regional, and global markets over the last decades that have affected small-scale producers in developing countries. Some of these changes, such as the changing food tastes of consumers in Europe, may seem distant from the challenges facing small-scale producers; however, the liberalisation and globalisation of markets means such changes increasingly affect producers even in distant markets. Before turning to the challenges faced by producers, it is important to spell out why markets and improved market access are important for small-scale producers and for rural development. There are three main reasons:

- *Poverty reduction:* most small-scale producers sell at least some produce on the market and rely on markets for some of their income. Helping small-scale producers access markets and get better prices for their produce therefore can increase household income and make an important contribution to reducing material poverty.
- *Empowerment and self-reliance:* if producers are able to access markets and receive a good price for their produce then they can use their own resources to trade their way out of poverty rather than relying on external assistance.
- *Pro-poor economic growth:* if significant numbers of small-scale producers increase their income from selling their produce on the market, this can promote growth in the rural economy as increased income leads to increased demand for labour, food, services, and consumer goods.[3]

Although markets have the potential to reduce poverty, create self-reliance, and drive pro-poor growth, all too often markets seem to be part of the problem rather than a potential solution. This is because in the real world markets fall far short of the efficient and effective means of exchange discussed in economic textbooks. Markets are often not competitive and are frequently dominated by a few powerful players. In poor rural economies, markets are often weak or they fail altogether because the cost and risks of participating in the market are too high. However, while there are clearly significant problems in many markets and problems with the global system of trade, avoiding markets is not a viable livelihood strategy for the majority of small-scale producers. Instead the challenge is to create a more level playing field for small-scale producers, i.e. to enable them to compete on a more equal basis, and to help them become more powerful market actors, by developing their capacity to compete in the market *and* by advocating for fairer trade systems and market structures that are not biased against small-scale producers in developing countries.

The market challenges presented below involve obvious examples of market failure but also challenges created by highly competitive markets in which small-scale producers are disadvantaged by their size, lack of resources, and isolation. These generic disadvantages include:

- limited land and capital and difficult environmental conditions that constrain production;
- geographical dispersion;
- low levels of literacy, poor health, and social and political marginalisation;
- weak transport and communications infrastructure that raises costs and lowers the prices received by producers;
- social and cultural constraints regarding acceptable gender roles and behaviour.

These challenges are described in detail in other material and we will not discuss them further here. However, it is important to keep these generic challenges in mind throughout this guide.

Below, we will consider the challenges posed by three different developments in global markets: market liberalisation; trends in local and global food markets; and changes in market chains (see Box 2.1 for an explanation of market or supply chains).

Box 2.1: Market or supply chains

A market or supply chain is a chain of economic actors, including producers, processors, traders and retailers, who each play a part in getting a product from the production stage to the consumer (see diagram below). Most market chains are made up of many independent actors who trade the product in separate markets at each stage of the chain. Most products are traded through more than one market or supply chain.

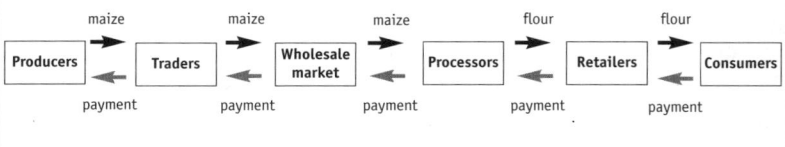

Market liberalisation[4]

Until the 1980s, the state in many developing countries intervened in rural markets to stabilise market prices, subsidise agricultural inputs, and provide agricultural marketing services. To achieve this, many states created marketing boards and rural co-operatives to co-ordinate agricultural production and control important markets. One of the main aims of these policies was to transfer resources from the agricultural sector to support industrialisation, and many states therefore imposed heavy taxes on agriculture despite the services they were providing to producers. The impact of these policies was mixed: in some countries the interventions were associated with very significant agricultural growth, as in parts of Asia where agricultural growth was faster than population growth and led to a dramatic fall in poverty. In many other regions the policies contributed little to growth and in sub-Saharan Africa, for example, per capita agricultural production declined by around 1 per cent between 1960 and 1980.[5]

By the early 1980s, a fundamental change in economic and development policy had taken place in the North. Evidence of poor economic performance in many developing countries, the rising costs of marketing boards (made worse by the oil shocks in the 1970s), and the rise of neo-liberalism, which saw state intervention as an enemy of growth, all led to a new drive for market-oriented growth and trade liberalisation.[6] State intervention in rural markets was now seen as a barrier to growth, and over the next two decades, market reform imposed by donors led to the closure of many marketing boards and the withdrawal of most agricultural marketing services provided by the state. Many donors reduced their support for agricultural services and between 1987 and 1998, for example, the total value of aid to agriculture fell by almost 70 per cent.[7]

Some of these policy changes had a positive effect on rural production. For example, in Ghana, improved economic management and devaluation of the currency almost doubled real producer prices of export crops.[8] However, these gains mostly benefited small-scale producers producing export crops and were often too small to compensate for the continued fall in commodity prices. Furthermore, market-oriented growth policies often had a negative impact on rural markets, especially food markets, as the private sector often did not fill the gap left by the state in the provision of agricultural marketing services. As a result many small-scale producers were faced with 'thin' markets (see Box 2.2), and had to cope without access to reliable and profitable input and output markets. This has had a particular impact on women, who are often responsible for food production and processing within the household. Meanwhile, the widespread reduction of state social services has often increased women's care burden and further limited their capacity to produce and market a surplus.

There are various reasons why private-sector service providers have been reluctant to enter poor rural markets and we will look at one important explanation here. According to this view, private companies are reluctant to provide marketing services, especially in food markets, because the costs and risks of doing business there are too high.[10] These costs are called 'transaction costs' and include the costs and risks involved in searching for buyers and sellers (search costs), the cost of assessing the quality and other characteristics of a product, and the costs of negotiating

Box 2.2: 'Thin' markets[9]

A 'thin' market is a market with a low volume of trade or a low number of transactions. For example, a 'thin' maize market means that only a small amount of maize is traded in a particular region. In a thin market, small-scale producers may have to wait for many days before a trader comes to their door, and if they take their maize to the local market they may only find a single buyer. This gives traders a strong bargaining position because small-scale producers have no other marketing option. But it also creates costs and risks for traders because they have to invest a lot of time searching for many farmers, who only sell small quantities. In thin markets, even a small increase in production and sales can have a big effect on prices, which adds to the risks faced by producers and traders. Because of the high risks there is often little incentive for traders or shopkeepers to provide services to producers to promote increased production.

a contract and making sure it is honoured. In thin markets, where transport and communications infrastructure is poor and law enforcement is weak, transaction costs can be so high that it is not worth doing business at all. As a result you get a vicious circle of under-investment: high transaction costs limit investment in the market and, as a result the volume and frequency of trade remains small, leading to high transaction costs and risks.[11]

As this vicious circle is caused by failures in the market, we cannot expect the market to produce a solution. What is needed is some kind of non-market intervention that can reduce the costs and risks of doing business so that all the actors in the market chain have the ability and confidence to invest. One way of achieving this is to reduce the risks of doing business by co-ordinating the investments of all these actors so that they all invest at the same time. For example, shopkeepers invest in supplying agricultural inputs, farmers invest in increased surplus production, traders invest in improved transport facilities, and investors invest in processing plants. In the past, marketing boards often performed this role by co-ordinating marketing services within a single structure: the board provided inputs to farmers and guaranteed to purchase their outputs. Although there were other problems associated with these agencies, it is important to recognise the significant role they often played in co-ordination investments in poor rural markets. In today's liberalised markets, there is often no one to co-ordinate investments among different actors in the market, especially in food markets, and as a result markets often remain weak. Sometimes, NGOs try to play a co-ordinating role on a small scale by linking producers and buyers, but these efforts tend to have a limited impact: poor rural markets often require co-ordination on a much larger scale and by an agency that has more influence and authority.

Another important dimension of market liberalisation affecting small-scale producers since the early 1980s is trade liberalisation.[12] To qualify for financial assistance from donors, developing countries have had to open up their markets to international trade by lowering trade barriers. For example, between 1980 and the end of the 1990s, average trade tariffs in Latin America fell by over 60 per cent.[13] As developing countries have opened their markets, small-scale producers have faced growing competition from commercial producers around the world, including subsidised producers in industrialised countries. While developing countries have reduced their trade barriers and cut back agricultural services, producers in industrialised countries continue to benefit from large subsidies and protected markets. European farmers, for example, received on average $16,000 in annual subsidies between 1998 and 2000.[14] These subsidies lead to over-production and the resulting surpluses are usually sold in the world market at prices well below the cost of production, depressing world prices for many products produced by small-scale producers in developing countries. The USA, for example, accounts for half the world's maize exports, but exports its maize at 20 per cent less than the actual cost of production.[15] On top of these subsidies, Northern countries protect their own markets through taxes on imports that rise with the level of processing and non-tariff barriers, such as health and food-safety standards and seasonal import restrictions.

In the face of these challenges, regional trade can offer more attractive trade options for developing countries. Trade among developing countries has increased significantly over the last decades, accounting for 40 per cent of developing-country exports in 1999.[16] While regional trade agreements (RTAs) among developing countries, such as COMESA (Common Market for Eastern and Southern Africa), can promote increased South–South trade, RTAs increasingly involve agreements between industrialised and developing countries, such as NAFTA (North America Free Trade Agreement) or the EU's Economic Partnership Agreements. These North–South agreements require developing countries to open up their markets in return for preferential access to US or EU markets, and may weaken existing South–South trade agreements. For example, under NAFTA, Mexican smallholder farmers, whose livelihoods depend on maize production, now have to compete with US maize farmers who receive an estimated $9bn a year in state support.[17] In today's global markets, small-scale producers therefore not only face significant constraints in their own markets but also have to contend with unfair competition in regional and world markets that are heavily biased in favour of producers in the North.

Trends in global markets

This section looks at trends in three different markets: the market for staple foods, such as rice or maize; the market for traditional cash crops, such as coffee and sugar; and finally the market for high-value products, such as fruit and vegetables.[18]

Growth in staple food markets

Although export markets present many opportunities for small-scale producers, they also involve significant obstacles and threats. For many small-scale producers, domestic and regional food markets may therefore present a more realistic market opportunity. Demand for food staples, such as maize, rice, and other cereals, is expected to increase significantly in developing countries over the coming decades. For example, domestic demand for food products in sub-Saharan Africa, at $50bn, is almost four times as big as total agricultural exports from the region.[19] Furthermore, the majority of rural poor people already produce staple foods, and the access barriers to these food markets are low, compared with agricultural export markets. However, the low value of staple foods also creates challenges for small-scale producers: not only are agricultural services for staple food production often missing, but the low value of staple foods means that producers have to sell large quantities and keep their marketing costs very low to make a profit. Furthermore, staple food markets are often unpredictable and risky as a result of uncertain weather conditions, inconsistent state interventions in the market, and food aid. Despite these challenges, domestic and regional staple food markets can represent an important market opportunity for small-scale producers if they can overcome some of the above challenges.

Challenges in traditional cash crop markets[20]

Many small-scale producers in developing countries depend on traditional cash crops such as coffee, tea, cocoa, rubber, and sugar. The price of these commodities has steadily fallen over the last 100 years. For example, current prices for tropical products are only around 15 per cent of the prevailing prices in 1980.[21] This fall has been caused by a combination of factors, including slow growth in demand (unlike manufactured or processed products, the demand for traditional cash crops does not rise as countries become wealthier) and increased global production since the 1980s, in particular since the end of International Commodity Agreements that controlled production. To make matters worse, these markets are increasingly dominated by a handful of powerful buyers or processing companies that are able to influence the prices received by producers. In response, many development organisations are calling for governments to introduce new commodity agreements to regulate global production, but even if this campaign is successful global prices are still likely to fall in the long term, as populations get wealthier. Small-scale producers of these cash crops therefore have to find new strategies to increase their income, including: adding value to their produce; differentiating their product (see the next section on high-value product markets); or diversifying production away from these commodities. Diversification may seem like an easy solution in theory but in practice small-scale producers have few other market opportunities, cannot afford to take on the risks involved in accessing new markets, and often do not have the skills and resources to switch production.

Growth in high-value product markets[22]

Changes in living standards, lifestyles, and working habits in Europe and North America and in large cities in developing countries have led to increased demand for:
- more healthy food such as fruit and vegetables;
- improved food quality and food safety, e.g. nuts that are the 'right' size and are free from any toxins;
- products that are produced in an environmentally sustainable or more ethical way, e.g. Fairtrade products or organic production that does not use chemicals;
- speciality products with unique characteristics, e.g. high-altitude, shade-grown coffee.

These changes have occurred largely in the markets of developed countries but they are also changing demand in middle-income countries and the large urban markets of many developing countries. In the past, agricultural products were mostly traded as commodities – a commodity is a product that is treated as a homogenous product, i.e. as if its quality was always the same, and so buyers and consumers are only interested in the quantity bought or sold. Over the last two decades this has changed as changes in consumer tastes and the huge increase in global trade has forced producers to differentiate their products in order to compete. Differentiation involves giving a product a unique identity that makes it different from the same product produced elsewhere. Today, producers who want to supply global markets cannot simply focus on production and assume there will be a market for their product. Instead, producers increasingly have to have a market orientation; in other words they have to identify what consumers want, produce a product that meets these demands, and maybe even differentiate their product in some way to compete in the market.

As consumers in industrialised countries have become more concerned about healthy eating and environmental and ethical issues, there has been rapid growth in demand for speciality products in 'niche' markets. Speciality products are products that have special characteristics based on their quality, origin, or how the product or the production process benefits producers or the environment. Organic and Fairtrade products are two examples of speciality products and the market for both has grown a lot in recent years. For example, global sales of organic bananas grew by more than 300 per cent between 1998 and 2002.[23] Fairtrade products are sold carrying the Fairtrade Mark, which guarantees that:

- the market chain for the product is certified against the Fairtrade Labelling Organisation's international Fairtrade standards (covering social, economic, and environmental issues); and
- a minimum price and premium for community-development projects have been paid to the producers.

Although these changes have created new opportunities for small-scale producers in high-value product markets, it has become increasingly difficult for small-scale producers to take advantage of them. Few small-scale producers have the skills, information, and resources to meet the standards and participate in the new types of marketing arrangements that are common in these markets (see Box 2.3). Furthermore, small-scale producers have to compete with large commercial farms in their own country that have many advantages in marketing, meeting standards, and accessing business services. It is much cheaper for a supermarket or their supplier to deal with one large commercial farm than with many small-scale producers and it is also easier and cheaper for commercial farms to meet supermarkets' quality and food-safety standards. To compete in these markets small-scale producers have to find ways to reduce their transaction and marketing costs and improve their access to services.

Box 2.3: Value chains[27]

The growth of supermarkets and the growing concentration in global food markets have resulted in fundamental changes in market chains. In the past, producers and later manufacturers controlled food-market chains and decided what was sold in the market. Today, the buyers – supermarket chains and multinational processing companies – control many global food-market chains, and they decide what can be sold on the market. As a result, many market chains are now managed in a very different way and are often called 'value chains', rather than market or supply chains, although the terms are often used interchangeably.

A value chain refers to a strategic network of independent businesses that work together to ensure that what is produced, the production process, and the quantity and timing meet the demands of retailers or processors. While market chains tend to be led by supply and involve limited exchange of information between actors in the chain, value chains are driven by demand and involve extensive exchange of information between businesses to communicate and enforce compliance with standards demanded by processors or retailers.
Value chains are buyer-driven and therefore frequently involve mechanisms to enforce buyers' standards, including supplier selection, auditing and inspections. Most high-value products are marketed through value chains.

Developments in global market chains

Market concentration[24]

Changes and new developments in global market chains have also created new challenges and opportunities for small-scale producers. All parts of the global food industry have experienced concentration over the last decades. Market concentration means that there are only a small number of companies operating at one stage in the market chain and these companies therefore can influence, if not control, prices. For example, five multinational groups control 69 per cent of the global coffee market and in Uganda, six international trading houses account for 80 per cent of coffee exports.[25] As we will see below, supermarkets also have considerable power in the market as a result of market concentration, which has weakened the position of producers.

However, it is important to recognise the difference between situations where a handful of buyers work together to exploit producers and cases where they work together to reduce the risks of doing business with small-scale producers. For example, a group of traders or companies may all agree to offer a price to producers that is below the actual market price: this is a clear case of exploitation. Alternatively, a processing company may want to provide seeds and training to farmers so they supply more and better quality produce to the processing plant. But the company risks losing the investment in these services if the farmers sell their crop to a different processor and so to reduce this risk the company may make an agreement with other processing companies only to buy crops from farmers they have provided services to. This kind of collaboration is often necessary to encourage growth in the market chain and does not have to be exploitative.[26]

Supermarkets[28]

As noted above, in most industrialised countries, food retail markets are dominated by a small number of large supermarket chains. For example, in the UK, the top four supermarkets accounted for almost 75 per cent of food sales in 2000.[29] This has had a significant effect on global fruit and vegetable market chains, as supermarkets account for a large share of fresh produce sold in many industrialised countries and increasingly also in many developing countries. Initially, the supermarkets bought fresh fruit and vegetables from wholesalers, but these wholesalers were not able to satisfy the supermarkets' growing demand for products that met their quality, food-safety, and traceability standards (traceability is the ability to identify exactly where, e.g. from which farm, a product has come from). Supermarkets therefore began to develop longer-term contracts with a

> **Box 2.4: Grades and standards**
>
> Grades and standards (G&S) include technical specifications, definitions, and systems for sorting a product into different quality, size, or other classes. For example, G&S for apples may include minimum quality requirements for all apples and three grades of apples, based on shape, size, and how many visible defects there are on the skin. In the past, most G&S focused on the characteristics of a product once it reached a certain stage in the market chain. Today, G&S increasingly focus on process standards, which focus on how a product is produced, processed, or marketed and not just on the quality of the final product.

small number of specialist suppliers, who also began to focus on a small number of their own suppliers, i.e. exporters in developing countries, who had the capacity to satisfy supermarkets' demands (see Box 2.4 on grades and standards).

Supermarket expansion has also had a big impact in developing countries, in particular in Latin America and East Asia where supermarkets now dominate retail markets. For example, supermarkets occupied 50–60 per cent of food retail in Latin America in 2000 and are growing fast in East and South-East Asia.[30] However, even in urban markets in Latin America, supermarkets only account for 25 per cent of the fresh food sector.[31] Supermarkets are also beginning to gain ground in Eastern and Southern Africa, although outside of South Africa and major urban centres there are few signs that traditional marketing channels, especially for fresh produce, are losing ground to supermarkets. Across the globe supermarkets therefore represent a growing challenge and an important market opportunity for small-scale producers supplying urban markets.

New product standards[32]

In the past, grades and standards were established by public authorities to make trade easier. Over the last decade there has been a rise of private standards established by groups of retailers in the EU and increasingly also by individual supermarket chains and other large companies. For example, to compete with other supermarkets and to satisfy their consumers, some supermarkets have introduced their own quality, food-safety, and traceability standards. These standards increasingly focus on the process of production rather than just the characteristics of the end product, because it is cheaper to control food quality and safety at the production stage rather than later in the value chain. This focus on the production process has also led to a big emphasis on traceability.

Box 2.5: Certification

Certification is a system that allows producers and companies to demonstrate to buyers and consumers that they have met certain quality, safety, or other standards. Most certification systems are run by independent organisations, which audit the producer or production process and provide a certificate confirming that the standards have been met. For example, to prove that they have met EurepGAP standards, producers need to be certified by a registered certification company. The Fairtrade Labelling Organisation also uses a certification system to demonstrate to consumers that a Fairtrade product has met the internationally agreed Fairtrade standards.

In addition to the standards established by individual companies, many supermarkets and global suppliers also require producers to implement collective standards such as the HACCP (Hazard Analysis Critical Control Points) methodology, a widely used monitoring system to control food-safety standards, or the EurepGAP farm certification standards, set up by a private body of retailers and their global suppliers.

To be certified against these standards, small-scale producers need to have considerable resources to invest in improved production processes, monitoring systems, and certification (Box 2.5). As few small-scale producers have this capacity, they risk growing exclusion from these markets, as supermarkets and their suppliers prefer to deal with large commercial producers, who are perceived to be more reliable and cheaper to deal with.

Contract farming[33]

In value chains, suppliers and processing companies increasingly make contractual agreements with producers in order to reduce their risks and guarantee that the produce meets the necessary standards. In a contract farming arrangement, exporters or processing companies make an advance contract with producers in which they agree to supply a specified quantity and quality of produce at harvest time, for an agreed price. An outgrower scheme is a similar system set up by a commercial farm to get small-scale producers to supply additional products to the farm. Both these schemes generally work through groups of farmers, which are often set up by the commercial farm or company to reduce its transaction costs. If they are confident that the producers will honour the contract, farms or companies often provide inputs on credit and extension services to the producers and then deduct the cost of these services from their payment for the crop. Contract farming schemes can provide a valuable marketing channel for small-scale producers and improve their access to important agricultural services that can also be used on their food crops.

However, because it is often more risky and expensive for suppliers to make contracts with small-scale producers, they are often excluded from such schemes. Unless producers have alternative marketing options and the ability to negotiate and enforce fair contracts, contract farming arrangements can trap producers in exploitative trade relationships that can lead to rising indebtedness and dependency and unsustainable farming practices. Women producers may find it particularly difficult to participate in contract farming arrangements as household duties may prevent them from delivering produce at the required time or to distant purchase points. Men therefore often manage product sales under such contracts, thereby reducing women's control over these transactions.

Summary: challenges to small-scale producers

Changes in local, regional, and global markets have created many market opportunities for small-scale producers but their ability to take advantage of these opportunities is heavily constrained by:

- a lack of capital, assets, skills, and information to compete in buyer-driven markets;
- high business costs in relation to the small size of their business;
- limited access to affordable and reliable services necessary to raise productivity and improve quality;
- weak bargaining position in local and global markets controlled by buyers;
- limited influence on local, national, and global policies and government practices that affect the markets they depend on for their livelihoods.

To overcome these challenges, small-scale producers need to develop their capacity to compete in the market, access external resources, and increase their bargaining power and influence. On their own, there is often little that individual small-scale producers can do to overcome these challenges – but what if they decide to co-operate and combine their resources to face the market together? The next chapter considers the benefits and costs of collective action.

3 | The rationale for producer organisations

POs can help small-scale producers improve their position in the market and overcome at least some of the challenges identified in the previous chapter in four basic ways:

1. *Increased scale:* POs bring together the business activities of many individual small-scale producers and thereby increase the overall scale of their joint business activities. This increased scale can lower small-scale producers' business costs, enable them to supply the quantity, quality, and consistency demanded by buyers, and increase their bargaining power and influence in the market. However, POs may have to reach a certain minimum size before the scale of their marketing activities gives them real bargaining power and enables them to compete with large, commercial producers.

2. *Intermediation:* POs act as an intermediary or link between individual producers, on the one hand, and buyers or service providers, on the other. Instead of having to do business with many individual and dispersed producers, buyers or service providers can deal with a single organisation and thereby reduce their transaction costs. However, co-operation within a PO also creates additional management costs and if a PO is not managed efficiently these costs may be greater than the benefits.

3. *Specialisation:* POs enable small-scale producers to pool their resources and then divide their labour between the different tasks involved in the business. This specialisation can enable POs to use their labour more efficiently, develop expertise in key areas, and free up members' time for other things.

4. *Co-operation:* the very process of working together can create solidarity and develop confidence among small-scale producers, enabling them to face the risks and challenges of the market and increase their influence on local policies and practices that affect their markets.

POs may have limited benefits if there are more fundamental problems with the way markets are structured. For example, POs alone can do little to redress the market power of supermarkets or overcome market failures in thin markets. POs are increasingly *necessary* for small-scale producers to have a chance of competing in and benefiting from the market, but POs are not always *sufficient* to achieve these aims. We will return to these important constraints after considering the main benefits of POs in the next section.

The potential benefits of collective action

Lower costs

One of the main benefits of POs is lower marketing costs as a result of economies of scale (see Box 3.1). For example, in Albania the members of a vine-growers co-operative used to process their wine individually but they have now generated economies of scale by investing in a single, high-quality wine-processing plant. In India, a co-operative-owned cotton-marketing company has generated economies of scale by buying agricultural inputs for its members in large quantities, at lower prices.

When small-scale producers combine their produce for sale it reduces the transaction costs for both the producers and the buyers. Instead of each producer spending time finding a buyer and negotiating a price, only one or two members do this on behalf of the whole group. For buyers, instead of spending a lot of time negotiating with individual producers over small quantities, they can negotiate once for a large quantity. These lower transaction costs mean that small-scale producers can often negotiate higher prices for the products they sell and lower prices for inputs. Particularly in thin markets, where individual producers and traders have to spend significant time searching for each other, POs can reduce these search costs and thereby encourage other actors to invest in the market chain.

Box 3.1: Economies of scale

Economies of scale are reductions in the cost of producing or marketing a unit of a product (e.g. one kilogram of coffee beans) as a result of increasing the overall scale of production or marketing. Production, processing, and marketing activities involve fixed costs, such as tractors, processing equipment, or storage facilities, and these costs fall for each unit produced, processed, or marketed as the overall scale of the activity increases.

Improved market reach

Many small-scale producers are unable to get a good price for their produce because they are unable to access other markets, further along the market or value chain, where prices are higher. Because they have no choice, small-scale producers have to accept the price that traders offer them locally. In such cases, collective action can enable small-scale producers to access other markets by combining their produce to reach the scale necessary to deal with buyers in other markets, or by processing their produce to access higher value markets at a later stage in the chain. For example, Asprepatía, an association in Colombia, has enabled producers to bulk and sell their produce directly to the wholesale market at better prices, rather than selling individually to local traders. POs can therefore provide a simple means of bypassing intermediaries in the market, such as local traders. However, this strategy only works if these intermediaries really are exploiting producers and are making big profits without adding much value to the product. In many cases, local traders only make a small profit because of the high transaction costs of doing business in poor rural areas and, in this case, POs may find it difficult to compete with them. By travelling together or organising a secure means of transport, POs can also enable women to access markets (which is sometimes difficult for them due to safety concerns or social norms that make it unacceptable for women to travel on their own).

Increased bargaining power

Collective action can increase small-scale producers' bargaining power (see Box 3.2) in various ways. By bulking and improving the quality of their product or by spreading production between individual members over the whole season, producers can meet the precise demands of buyers and therefore negotiate better prices. For example, Agrolempa, a limited company owned by an association of fruit and vegetable producers in El Salvador, has been able to access more demanding national markets by combining the produce of its member owners and other producers in the region, to meet the quantities demanded by buyers. Economies of scale can make it easier for a PO to invest in processing, storage, or transport facilities that can give members the ability to choose when and where to sell their products. For example, a vine growers' co-operative in Albania enabled producers to invest in better processing equipment that preserved their wine for longer and allowed producers to access markets outside the local area.

> **Box 3.2: Bargaining power**
>
> Bargaining power is the ability to influence the price or terms of a business transaction. Even if buyers cannot offer higher prices, bargaining power can enable producers to negotiate better terms, such as a long-term supply agreement or access to business services. Bargaining power depends on many different factors but the most important are scarcity, the availability of alternative marketing options, and market information:
>
> - *Scarcity*: if a product is in short supply compared to the demand for the product then the producer is usually in a strong bargaining position. However, scarcity often only applies to products with certain characteristics. For example, there may be hundreds of producers selling tomatoes to a wholesale market but very few of them deliver tomatoes in the quantity and quality favoured by traders. In this case, only the producers that can meet these expectations have a product that is in short supply and will be able to negotiate better prices.
>
> - *Alternative marketing options*: even if producers are selling a product that is in short supply, they will still be in a weak bargaining position if they do not have alternative marketing options. This situation may arise in thin rural markets where there are few traders, and producers do not have adequate transport or storage facilities.
>
> - *Market information*: access to accurate information about market prices and conditions can help producers avoid exploitation by buyers and negotiate a fair price.

In buyer-driven market chains, POs can create 'countervailing' power that provides some balance to the power of buyers. For example, the association in Colombia, mentioned above, controlled a large share of the local market and was therefore able to negotiate better prices from wholesalers and force local traders to pay much higher prices. Countervailing power can be particularly important when producers are either marketing perishable products, like fruit or milk that go bad quickly, or if they have invested in expensive processing equipment that cannot be used for other purposes. In both cases the producers' bargaining position is weak: in the first case, because producers have to sell their product quickly, i.e. before it goes bad, which forces them to accept lower prices; in the second case, the large investment in equipment forces producers to continue production even if they get low prices. In such cases, producers can sometimes create countervailing power and improve their bargaining position by forming a large PO that buyers have to do business with. This was one of the main reasons for the creation of POs in Europe and the USA in the last century:[34] to compete in buyer-driven markets, farmers have had to invest in processing equipment to add value to their products, but these investments can weaken their bargaining position and so farmers form POs to create countervailing power.

Improved access to services

POs can improve small-scale producers' access to services in two ways. Firstly, the lower transaction costs and economies of scale involved in providing services to groups rather than to individual producers makes it much cheaper and easier for businesses and service providers to work with small-scale producers. For example, members of UCASN, an association of producers in Mozambique, have been able to access input and extension services from exporters which are otherwise unavailable. Secondly, organised groups of producers, especially if they are legally registered, are likely to have greater credibility and a higher profile than individual producers. This makes it much easier for service providers to identify and work with producers and can also improve access to financial services, as rural banks are more likely to offer credit to a registered organisation than to individual farmers. In some cases, large POs may also be able to provide services to their members, particularly in markets where access to appropriate services is limited or non-existent. However, this is a high-risk strategy, as the PO has to recover the costs of providing these services to remain a viable business. For example, some West African POs employ extension staff to support their members in organic cotton production but they have to raise their sale prices on average by 20 per cent to recover the costs of the extension service.

Incentives and opportunities for value adding

Collective action does not itself enable small-scale producers to engage in processing activities and add value to their produce. However, the economies of scale created by POs, the improved market reach, and access to services can all help producers to mobilise the resources and develop the level of expertise necessary to carry out such activities successfully. Once a PO has enabled producers to access markets that offer higher prices for high-quality products, the producers will have a strong incentive to improve the quality and add value to their produce. For example, once the members of an olive-oil co-operative in Palestine had developed links to high-value olive-oil markets in Europe, there was a strong incentive for members to improve the quality of their oil by managing the pressing process more effectively. Processing activities often require significant investments in equipment, which are too expensive and risky for individual producers. POs can also enable producers to access the capital necessary to invest in processing equipment, while also sharing the risk of the investment between many producers.

Increased confidence

Small-scale producers often lack the confidence, skills, and experience to engage successfully in the market. Collective action can make a big difference, as producers no longer have to rely on their own skills and resources and do not have to face the risks of engaging in the market on their own. There is strength and solidarity in working as a group, which can enable small-scale producers, in particular women or members of other marginalised groups, to take risks and gain confidence in the market. As a member of COMUCAP, an association of rural women in Honduras, explained, 'Thanks to COMUCAP, we have learned that we have the right to be free and to speak out. Now we can help our husbands, and we can earn money for the household. People in the community admire us now. We have won respect from men.'. As this quote demonstrates, producers gain confidence from the increased income and independence generated by collective marketing activities.

Increased influence

Large POs can provide the platform for producers to promote their interests and influence policies in the local, national, and even international environment that affect their business and livelihood. For example, NASFAM, an association of smallholder farmers in Malawi, has successfully lobbied the government for tax concessions on smallholder tobacco sales while the Guyana Rice Producers' Association persuaded millers and exporters to provide timely payments to producers. Collective action through a PO can also mobilise producers to do something about other problems that affect the wider community. When members of the Guyana Rice Producers' Association were affected by a natural disaster, the association mobilised resources to provide relief to the whole community.

Risks and costs of collective action

Collective action is no magic solution to the challenges small-scale producers face in the market. POs also involve potential challenges that have to be overcome and internal costs that have to be met before their members are likely to gain more than they have invested in the organisation. And even if POs develop and become successful businesses, they can still be small players in national and global markets controlled by powerful interests. The following section identifies some of the main risks and costs of collective action.

Governance and trust

Poor governance and the breakdown of trust between members, leaders, and managers is one of the main reasons POs run into difficulties or collapse. Managing a group of producers with different priorities is a difficult task, especially when POs become larger. A lot of time and resources have to be spent on consulting with members, communicating between the different levels of the organisation, and developing a consensus on important issues. Sometimes this trust and commitment or 'social capital' already exists among members when the PO is formed, but often POs have to invest considerable time to develop and then maintain this social capital as the organisation grows. While social capital within the PO is critical to its sustainability, it can also work against the interests of the least powerful members within the PO or of other community members who are not participating in the PO. Like any organisation, POs can easily be used by local elites to promote their own interests and exert power over poorer and less powerful producers.

Internal transaction costs

While POs can reduce the transaction costs for buyers and service providers, they create new transaction costs within the organisation. For example, POs often purchase and distribute inputs to members, collect produce from individual members, pay them, and then collect and transport this produce for sale to a buyer. These internal transactions involve costs that can be very high, especially if the PO is not managed efficiently and there are delays in distributing inputs or paying members. In this case, POs risk losing business to traders who may be able to offer better prices to members than the PO can, because of lower operating costs. For example, in the past some members of NASFAM have sold their produce to traders rather than to NASFAM because of delays in NASFAM's payment system.

Free riding

To achieve economies of scale most POs combine the produce of their members for processing or marketing. Although this process is essential for the success of the PO it also involves potential risks and losses for individual members. For example, some members of the vine growers' co-operative in Albania were reluctant to switch to collective wine processing because they feared that the quality of the wine would be reduced by poorer quality grapes supplied by other members. They even feared that a collective processing system could encourage some members to invest less time in managing their vines because they could reap the benefits from the higher quality grapes supplied by other members. This type of behaviour is called 'free riding' as some members benefit from the efforts or investments made by others. In Kenya, for example, an association of wood carvers almost went out of business because it did not have a system that rewarded carvers for the quality of their products and so the most skilled carvers gradually left the association. POs need to develop systems to discourage free riding by creating incentives for all members to invest in the business.

Increased profile

As formal or informal organisations of producers, POs raise the profile of producers in the market and in the political arena. While this can bring many benefits in terms of improved access to services, the increased profile can also create problems and increase business costs. For example, the association Agrolempa in El Salvador is formally registered as a business and therefore has to pay taxes. Many of its competitors, however, are informal traders who do not pay taxes and therefore can offer attractive prices to Agrolempa's members. In some regions, such as parts of sub-Saharan Africa, where there is a history of political control of co-operatives, successful POs may attract unwanted attention from the authorities that may threaten their business.

Summary: the benefits and costs of POs

While collective action in itself cannot solve all the competitive and structural challenges faced by small-scale producers, POs can create:

- an intermediary and larger business that enables small-scale producers to compete more effectively in the market and increase their bargaining power;
- a platform for producers to promote and defend their interests; and
- a channel through which support and investment can be provided to small-scale producers more efficiently and effectively.

POs involve a critical and sometimes delicate balance between the benefits of co-operation and additional costs and potential risks created by such activities. In practice, the balance between these benefits and costs determines the profitability of a PO and therefore its survival: unless a PO can provide services to its members at attractive prices and cover the costs of these services, its members will access alternative service providers and, sooner or later, the PO will go out of business.

4 | Who benefits from producer organisations?

In recent years, POs have become a very popular subject in rural development and today it is difficult to find a policy paper on rural development that does not encourage promoting POs. It is therefore important to take a step back and examine who really benefits from POs. Our main question in this chapter is whether POs can help all small-scale producers, including the poorest producers, or whether they usually only work for better-off small-scale producers. But we also need to ask whether the benefits of POs extend beyond the members to reach their families, other producers, and the wider community. We will consider these two questions in turn below.

Can POs benefit all small-scale producers?

According to our definition in the first chapter, POs are rural businesses engaged in collective marketing activities. Most POs focus on collective output marketing activities, and to participate in this activity producers need to be able to produce a surplus. This is an obvious point but this condition immediately excludes large numbers of rural producers from directly benefiting from POs. In many countries a large proportion of rural producers are subsistence producers who do not have the capacity to produce a reliable surplus for the market. For example, in Ethiopia around 60 per cent of the rural population rely on subsistence production and have insufficient land and resources to produce a surplus for the market.[35] For these producers, a PO offers few immediate advantages although other types of collective action, such as community-based organisations, may help them mobilise resources and assistance to address more fundamental problems in the community. A simple answer to our first question therefore is that POs, as defined in this guide, will often not directly benefit a significant number of small-scale producers who are unable to produce a reliable surplus. This conclusion is supported by research findings and historical evidence that suggest that POs are usually set up by better-off small-scale producers.[36] But there are further reasons why it is often difficult for poorer small-scale producers to participate in POs. These are:

1. Poorer small-scale producers with few assets, limited skills, and unfavourable environmental conditions will find it difficult to produce the quantities of low-value staples required for a PO to compete in a volume market but, equally, will struggle to produce high-value products, such as fruit and vegetables, that consistently meet the quality required for a PO to compete in high-value product markets.

2. The demands of household caring duties mean women are usually 'time-poor' and may therefore not have the time to participate in a PO. Women may also be excluded from participation in POs due to cultural constraints or because they have limited access to cash income, which may limit their ability to pay membership fees and invest in the business.

3. Occasional market sales can provide a means for poor producers to diversify their income and spread their risk but this is different from marketing a surplus as part of a market-oriented business. To succeed in the market POs often have to take risks that many poorer small-scale producers may be unable or unwilling to take.

4. It often takes a number of years before a PO breaks even and is able to pay its members prices that are higher than those offered by other traders. Until it reaches this point, members may have to make additional investments in the PO without receiving any benefits but poorer small-scale producers often do not have the resources to make this kind of sacrifice.

5. Many POs do not pay members immediately for their produce but poorer small-scale producers often need cash immediately and this may prevent them from participating in a PO. For example, when a co-operative in Albania began producing and marketing wine collectively, some poorer producers left the organisation, as they could not afford to wait additional weeks until the co-operative could pay them for its sales.

6. PO membership involves different types of cost, including membership fees or share purchases. These costs may often be too high for small-scale producers, especially women producers, with limited cash. For example, poor coffee producers in Uganda were unable to join a coffee co-operative that could offer them better prices because they could not afford to pay the membership fee and buy shares in the co-operative.

7. Sometimes POs are formed or controlled by local elites whose main aim is to control local market activities, in particular the marketing activities of poorer farmers.
8. The majority of the poorest small-scale producers live in poor, remote areas where markets tend to be thin and the challenges of developing a successful PO are much higher. As a result, there are often few successful POs in these areas that producers can join.

This list of barriers should dispel any illusions about POs as a straightforward development tool to help poor small-scale producers. Many of these challenges can be overcome with time and with significant external support. For example, NGOs can implement projects that help small-scale producers raise their productivity and produce higher quality products, and as POs develop and become stronger they can often find ways to extend their business and services to benefit poorer producers with less capacity. However, there is a danger that POs can become a means for external agencies to channel resources to small-scale producers, in an attempt to make POs more inclusive or to promote other development objectives within the wider community. However, such approaches risk dampening and even undermining the organisations' development and reducing the independence and entrepreneurialism of producers, on which POs' long-term success depends (see Chapter 7).

Do the benefits of POs extend beyond their members?

POs are sometimes criticised for being 'development islands' in which development and investment is concentrated, with limited benefit for the wider community. We therefore also need to consider to what extent POs benefit the families of members as well as the wider community.

We cannot assume that the whole household will necessarily share the benefits received by one family member participating in a PO, as this depends on the division of roles and the balance of power between members in the household, in particular between male and female members. For example, if a husband participates in a PO he may expect his wife (and children) to spend more time growing cash crops for sale through the PO. This may place considerable pressure on his wife who still has to perform the usual household duties, while the husband may gain more power within the household as a result of his cash-crop income. And while women's participation in a PO can increase their income, confidence, and independence, as demonstrated by COMUCAP in Honduras, participation in a PO will often add to their workload and may place more pressure on older children, particularly older female children who may be removed from school to look after younger siblings.

Within the wider community, people who are not PO members often benefit from services provided by POs. For example, Agrolempa in El Salvador also purchases fruit and vegetables from non-members who benefit from fair scales and lower transport costs. Successful POs may also contribute to growth in the rural economy that benefits all rural producers through increased demand for wage labour and other goods and services. For example, in Ethiopia, members of a successful farmer co-operative expanded their production and hired more workers, thus benefiting poorer producers in need of employment opportunities. POs create social networks that often extend beyond their membership. As a focal point within the community, POs can enable community members to meet, socialise, and discuss issues facing the community or local producers. Lastly, large POs or POs with considerable resources often implement social projects or provide social services in the local community. For example, NASFAM in Malawi funds small-scale community projects to improve rural infrastructure.

POs are producer-owned businesses that can help small-scale producers overcome the fundamental disadvantages they face in today's markets as a result of their size, lack of resources, and marginalisation. However, POs cannot work miracles and they should not be seen as an alternative way of transforming a poor rural community. In many cases, much greater investments and interventions by states, donors, and NGOs are required to address more fundamental constraints that prevent many small-scale producers from producing enough to feed their families, let alone to participate in demanding markets. The challenge for those working with POs is to find ways of maximising their benefits to members and their indirect benefits to the wider community without undermining their business. This is a central question we will consider in the rest of this book.

Summary: who benefits from POs?

To participate in and therefore benefit directly from POs, producers have to be able to produce a surplus that meets the demands of the target market and satisfies other conditions of membership. These requirements will often make it difficult if not impossible for large numbers of poorer small-scale producers, especially women, to participate in POs without prior or complementary interventions to improve rural infrastructure and develop the assets and skills of these producers. Non-members may nonetheless benefit indirectly from POs, through services offered to non-members, increased demand for labour, and social activities supported by POs. However, these benefits can be limited and patchy. To survive as a business, most POs will have to invest surplus resources back into the business during the early years of development, and few POs will therefore generate the resources to support social activities that benefit the wider community until much later in their development.

Part II | What Do Producer Organisations Look Like and How Do They Operate?

Orienting questions

What do POs do?
What legal forms do POs have and how are they structured internally?
How are POs managed and governed?
What types of business activities do POs get involved in?
What types of relationships can POs have with buyers or suppliers?
How do POs access market services?
What can POs do to influence their environment?
How do POs develop over time?

In Part I, we looked at the background to and rationale for POs. Part II takes a closer look at POs themselves and the questions listed above. As we look at each of these aspects we will consider what factors contribute to successful POs and what dangers and pitfalls POs need to avoid. Throughout this part we will draw on case studies of POs around the world to provide real examples of POs and how they operate.[37]

5 | Producer organisation activities and services

When producers come together to form a PO, often the initial aim is to work together and collectively perform the tasks individual members previously undertook on their own. As POs grow, these tasks are increasingly performed by employees working for the PO, as a service to the PO's members. A good place to begin our investigation into POs is to consider what POs actually do. Below we will provide a brief summary of some of the main activities and services provided by POs to their members, looking first at those activities and services that are directly connected with the PO's business before considering two other types of PO services. First, we will introduce our first case study of an association in El Salvador.

Case Study 1: Agrolempa, El Salvador

Agrolempa was established in San Vicente in El Salvador in 2001, as a rural association with a commercial trading company that is 100 per cent owned by the association. The farmers who formed the association had previously received support from a local NGO and an Oxfam project, funded by the European Union, which provided the start-up capital for the company. The aim of the association is to improve the livelihoods of small-scale producers by helping them to obtain better prices for their agricultural produce. It tries to achieve this by helping its members to improve the quality of their fruit and vegetables and by buying their produce and selling it directly to the hospital industry, supermarkets, caterers, processors, and wholesale markets. In this way it cuts out the traders who pay low prices to the producers. The association has around 60 members. Members are required to be smallholder farmers with their own land. The association elects a board of directors, which hires the managers of the company, and is responsible for monitoring their performance. Because the members and other local people do not have the skills and experience to manage the company, the board have from the beginning hired managers from outside the region who are committed to the objectives of the association. Each year the board decides what to do with any trading profits made by the company. In 2005, the board decided to distribute 80 per cent of profits to members, based on how much produce they had supplied to the company, and the remaining 20 per cent of profits was distributed equally to all members.

Agrolempa has become one of only three agricultural trading companies supplying the major institutional markets and the retail and catering trade in El Salvador. It has achieved this by focusing heavily on improving the quality of its members' fruit and vegetable production and by developing a quality-management system. To achieve the volume of supply and offer the range of produce demanded by hospital and supermarket contracts, Agrolempa has become a trading company, buying produce from members and from suppliers who are not members in the region and even in neighbouring countries. Although Agrolempa has developed a strong position in the market, the scale of its current business is still insufficient to cover all its costs. The association-owned company pays normal commercial tax rates while most of the informal traders it competes with do not. For these reasons, it has not always been able to pay its members better prices than the traders, who have frequently raised their prices to persuade members to sell to them. However, the association's members are very committed to Agrolempa and accept that it may take some years until the company is able to break even (without receiving external support) and reward their commitment with considerably better prices and dividends.

Business-oriented producer-organisation services

As we saw in the case study, Agrolempa provides a range of business-oriented services to its members. Some of the most common business-oriented activities and services provided by POs are listed below:

- *Input supply:* like Agrolempa, POs often buy inputs in bulk, at lower prices, and then supply them to their members. In fact, some POs are set up solely to provide agricultural inputs more cheaply to their members.

- *Production services:* as small-scale producers generally have limited assets and skills, POs frequently provide extension services and access to equipment, such as tractors, to help members increase their productivity and improve the quality of their produce. Agrolempa, for example, has provided training to its members to improve their cultivation practices.

- *Financial services:* access to cash loans and input credit is a very important service provided by many POs. Often these services are managed by an independent structure, as in the case of Agrolempa, where most of the current members are also members of a savings and credit co-operative.

- *Training:* in addition to extension training, many POs provide training in literacy, numeracy, basic accounting, and report keeping, in order to help members manage their own business activities better and improve their understanding of the PO's business.
- *Quality control:* to meet the demanding quality and food-safety standards of some markets, POs need to monitor and control the production process and the quality of the final product they sell. For example, NASFAM, a PO we will describe in Case Study 3, has set up a quality-control system to ensure its groundnuts meet European Union food-safety requirements.
- *Co-ordinating production:* to take advantage of different market opportunities and respond to the needs of buyers, POs have to co-ordinate the individual production of their members. For example, POs can meet the demand of buyers, who expect a continuous supply of fresh produce throughout the season, by organising members to plant their crops at different stages during the planting season.
- *Output marketing:* marketing members' produce is the core service provided by most POs. To do this successfully, POs have to perform a range of tasks, including analysing market information, identifying market opportunities, negotiating sales, collecting, storing and transporting produce, and, of course, paying members.
- *Processing:* some POs engage in processing activities in order to add value to their produce and access markets further along the market or value chain. Some of the POs we will encounter later in this book are involved in processing olives into olive oil, grapes into wine, and sugar cane into a brown sugar loaf called panela.
- *Trading:* some POs become traders, buying and selling produce from producers other than just their own members, in order to meet the quantity, variety, or consistency of supply demanded by certain markets. Agrolempa, for example, is involved in large-scale trading activities, as it cannot meet the demands of its target markets with the produce supplied by its members.
- *Retailing:* occasionally, some POs get involved in retailing activities. A small co-operative near Addis Ababa in Ethiopia, for example, has established a grocery shop through which it sells its members' fruit and vegetables, enabling them to get much better prices than they got previously in the local wholesale market.

Of course, most POs will only provide a small number of these services, based on the needs of their members, the demands of the market, and, most importantly, whether they can cover the costs of providing these services. As we will see in Chapter 8, POs can only survive if they provide services required by their members at a lower cost than their competitors. As many of these services, such as processing or trading, require large investments and significant skills and experience, POs sometimes use the services provided by independent service providers, for example to transport, process, store, or trade their produce. We will return to the role of market service providers in Chapter 9.

Other services

POs can provide additional services to their members that are not directly connected to their business. For example, Asprepatía, a Colombian PO described in Case Study 8, was established by producers who were campaigning against a planned sugar mill that threatened their livelihood. In Chapter 10 we will look at how POs try to defend and promote their members' interests in more detail.

Many POs also provide social services to their members and the wider community. For example, the women's association COMUCAP in Honduras was set up to raise awareness among women about their rights and address the problem of domestic violence. Over the last ten years, its members have established a number of successful enterprises, including organic coffee production and producing soap from aloe vera. COMUCAP continues to provide social services to women alongside its market services, but it has recently taken the difficult decision to manage the social and business activities under two separate structures. Although its social objectives have informed and driven all its activities, the management believe it is important to separate the two to prevent social concerns undermining the sustainability of its business activities.

As the example of COMUCAP illustrates, POs (and NGOs working with POs) often find it difficult to get the right balance between social and business objectives. In the long term, a PO can only provide services to its members, whether business or social services, if they develop a successful business that is financially sustainable and can generate the resources necessary to support both social and market services. As many POs even struggle to cover the costs of their market services, it is important to be realistic about their capacity to provide social services, unless these are funded by external grants. However, as COMUCAP's experience highlights, mixing grant-funded social activities and profit-oriented business activities within the same organisation can also create difficulties, and POs need to develop appropriate structures to manage these activities effectively.

Summary: PO activities and services

- POs can provide many different business-oriented services to their members but they often use market services provided by independent market service providers if they cannot themselves provide these services to their members, at a profit.
- POs sometimes provide social services to their members and the wider community. If social objectives drive business decisions they can undermine the PO's business. Social activities are therefore best managed separately from the PO's business.

6 | Producer organisation structure

This chapter identifies the most common legal and organisational structures adopted by POs and what implications these different structures have for producers and their collective businesses.

Legal structure

The legal structure or status of a PO describes what type of organisation it is according to the law. Sooner or later, most POs have to register their organisation with the authorities and at this point they can usually decide between different types of legal structure. This choice is important because the legal structure determines many important things in an organisation. The following is a list of ten critical issues, which are affected by the choice of legal structure:

- *Ownership:* can anyone own shares in the PO and can owners buy as many shares as they like?
- *Membership:* can anyone join the PO, including women and minority groups, or are there restrictions on membership? Is membership assigned to individual members or does it include other family members?
- *Voting rights:* who can make decisions within the PO and how are these decisions made?
- *Distribution of profits:* can business profits be distributed to members and, if yes, according to what principle?
- *Risk:* what happens if the business goes bankrupt? Who is liable for the business' debts?
- *Regulation:* how much freedom does the PO want to have to make its own rules and manage its affairs independently, without outside interference or useful external controls?

- *Credibility:* how much credibility will the PO have in the eyes of potential lenders, investors, and business partners?
- *Taxation:* how will the business be taxed?
- *Investment incentives:* what incentives will the PO provide to new and existing members to invest their resources in the business?
- *Share transfer:* can existing members sell their shares when they exit the organisation or are the PO's shares not tradable?

The most common legal structures that we will consider in this chapter are: informal organisations, associations, co-operatives, hybrid structures, and private companies. These structures are not defined in exactly the same way in every country and some structures may not exist at all in some countries. They are, however, the most common types of legal structure used by POs and the main features are likely to be similar in most countries. The individual characteristics of these five structures are listed in detail in Annex 4, with particular reference to the ten critical issues listed above. Below we will briefly summarise the main features and advantages and disadvantages of these five different structures but first we will introduce another case study about three Clam Clubs in southern Viet Nam.

Case Study 2: Clam Clubs, Viet Nam

Clams are not farmed but are raised in open coastal waters and therefore require supervision to prevent damage or theft before they are harvested. Since 2003, three Clam Clubs have been established in the coastal district of Tra Vinh province in southern Viet Nam. These were not the first attempts at collective clam-raising in the area. A group of well-off households had previously attempted to raise clams but had failed because the whole community did not support the initiative and so the participants were unable to prevent other people harvesting their clams.

In collaboration with the local authorities, Oxfam GB organised a series of meetings with local farmers to set up a collective clam-raising initiative. The clubs were established in three communities and all members had to contribute money to purchase baby clams. Poor members were able to borrow money for their contribution from a revolving fund set up by Oxfam GB. When the clams are sold the members repay their loan with a small amount of interest and the following season another group of poor members are able to borrow money from the fund. Initially, club members took turns to guard the clams but soon they decided to pay members from poor households to work as permanent guards. Oxfam GB also provided technical and management training for the clubs on how to organise and manage the clubs' activities. Exposure visits were organised to baby-clam suppliers, clam co-operatives, and local markets. There is strong demand for the clams and a lot of competition between the buyers, so the clubs are able to negotiate a good price. For this reason, the clubs do not

> make any agreements with the buyers before the harvest. The first harvest of clams in 2005 was a success and the clubs were able to sell the clams at a considerable profit. The profits were distributed to each member according to how much money they had invested at the start.
>
> The clubs are made up of around 60 members and have a formal structure with paid managers and a constitution. However, they are only registered locally with the district authorities as 'collaborative groups' and are therefore considered as informal organisations. The clubs are not expected to pay taxes but they have difficulties accessing credit because they are not registered as a business or co-operative.

Informal organisations

Informal organisations, according to this guide, are POs that are not formally registered and therefore do not have legal rights as an organisation. Like the Clam Clubs, many new POs start off as informal organisations and only register once the benefits of registration are greater than the additional costs and effort associated with registration. In some countries the laws governing POs are poorly defined or only permit certain types of structure that are not appropriate for small-scale producers and in such cases it may be easier for a PO to operate informally. In Viet Nam, co-operatives are the only legal structure for collective business but co-operatives have a lot of rules and regulations that are not suitable for a small clam-raising enterprise. If a PO is competing in an informal market without effective regulation, then a formally registered PO will often be at a disadvantage compared with informal traders and buyers, as in the case of Agrolempa in El Salvador (Case Study 1). However, informal organisations also have many disadvantages, including problems accessing market services, such as credit or technical assistance, and reduced credibility in the eyes of potential business partners.

Associations

An association is a membership organisation in which members participate to receive certain services and benefits. Many NGOs and community-based organisations are registered as associations but it is also a common legal structure for POs. For example, NASFAM, in Malawi (Case Study 3), is an association of smallholder farmers. The main advantages of associations are their independence, freedom, and flexibility. As the members of an association can decide how to structure and manage the organisation, they can create the structure and rules that suit their needs and circumstances. In many countries this independence is a critical factor: NASFAM, for example, chose to register as an association rather than as a co-operative because, according to the law in Malawi, a government official has to sit on the board of every co-operative. The main disadvantage of associations is that their structure is not really designed for business activities and in many countries associations are treated as non-profit organisations. This often means that associations are not permitted to distribute business profits to their members, and members are personally liable for the associations' debts. NASFAM and Agrolempa got around this problem by creating a separate private company, owned by the association, that can donate its profits to the association.

Co-operatives

Co-operatives have a long history and are probably the most widely recognised form of PO. There is an internationally recognised, traditional form of co-operative regulated by the International Co-operative Alliance (ICA). The main purpose of traditional co-operatives is to provide services to their members at a competitive price. Their most distinctive feature is a democratic form of ownership and control: all members have equal shares in the business, decision-making is based on the principle 'one member, one vote', and profits are distributed according to patronage, i.e. how much members use the co-operative's services. These features distinguish co-operatives from private companies where ownership, decision-making, and profit distribution is proportional to each member's investment in the business. The Palestinian olive-oil co-operatives, described in Case Study 5, are an example of a traditional co-operative.

Traditional co-operatives also have some disadvantages: like associations, co-operatives often have difficulties raising money for investment from their members. As all members have equal ownership and voting rights and the co-operative's profits are distributed according to patronage, there is little motivation for members to invest their own funds in the co-operative's business. While this is of little concern for many co-operatives, whose members do not have any surplus money to invest in the business, it can be a problem for more advanced organisations. Co-operatives are also quite heavy structures, i.e. they have many rules and regulations, which do not allow for much flexibility, and create additional internal administration costs. In many parts of the world producers are very suspicious of co-operatives because of negative experiences in the past with state-led co-operative-promotion programmes. As we saw from the example of NASFAM, many states still take a close interest in how co-operatives are run, which can lead to unwelcome government interference. In practice, governments may define any of these structures in ways that enable them to maintain some level of control over PO activities, which can weaken POs' ability to operate freely and independently.

Hybrid structures

A new legal structure has emerged in recent years in response to some of the disadvantages of co-operatives as well as the growing challenges producers face in markets driven by buyers. This new mixed or hybrid structure combines features of both traditional co-operatives and private companies. One example of such a structure is the so-called 'New Generation Cooperative' (NGC).[38] In contrast to traditional co-operatives, NGCs have closed membership, limited to a fixed number of members, and business profits and voting rights are distributed according to members' share of the business. This share is represented by fixed supply contracts that members have to buy when they join the co-operative. NGCs are therefore structured in a similar way to a private company and members have a strong incentive to invest in the business. Although these changes can address many of the problems associated with traditional co-operatives, most of these features will not be relevant to POs whose members have no money to invest, and which need to create big organisations to increase their bargaining power. However, some legal structures provide some flexibility in how to manage membership, voting rights, and so on, and new POs may be able to borrow some of these features to suit their purposes. For example, in Mozambique, each member of a new co-operative has been allocated one, two, or three votes at the general meeting, depending on how much they have invested in the business.

Private companies

The main purpose of a private company is to make a profit on the money invested by its owners, i.e. the company's shareholders and members. The main advantage of a private company is that its legal structure is designed for business activities and encourages investment by members and external investors. Private companies also have the advantage that they can have members and shareholders who are not active, i.e. who are not producers, in the case of POs. This option can provide an important means of raising funds, as investors are more likely to invest in a business if they also gain some control over how the business is run. However, this arrangement could cause problems for our definition of POs in Part I, which suggested that POs should be owned and controlled by small-scale producers. However, if this is only a temporary arrangement designed to overcome specific financial or management constraints, it need not conflict with our definition. Private companies also have a number of disadvantages, which can make them an unsuitable structure for collective businesses run by small-scale producers. As decision-making is based on ownership, private companies are usually run according to the interests of the wealthiest members, which may disadvantage poorer members. In many countries there is also a limit on the number of owners a private company can have, so this structure may only be suitable for small POs with a small number of members. However, as we saw above, private companies can be owned by co-operatives and associations, which overcomes this constraint. Unlike co-operatives and associations, private companies are taxed on their profits, which can be a heavy burden for small-scale producers, especially if they are competing in an informal market.

Multi-level and mixed structures

As POs develop and their membership grows, they often become difficult to manage in a single organisation. As we noted in Part I, for POs to be successful it is important that there is trust between the members of the organisation. This is only possible if the group is small enough to allow members to communicate with each other on a regular basis and if the members live close to each other. Most studies of POs suggest that the ideal size of such groups is between 15 and 30 members, not any larger. However, in Part I we also suggested that small-scale producers have to increase the scale of their business in order to increase their bargaining power and compete in the market. To combine both these needs – small groups *and* increased scale – POs often bring together a number of small, first-level organisations, under a new, 'second-level' organisation, which represents and provides services to these smaller POs. In some cases, these second-level organisations may even come together to create a 'third-level' organisation, as illustrated in Figure 6.1.

Figure 6.1: A three-level producer organisation structure

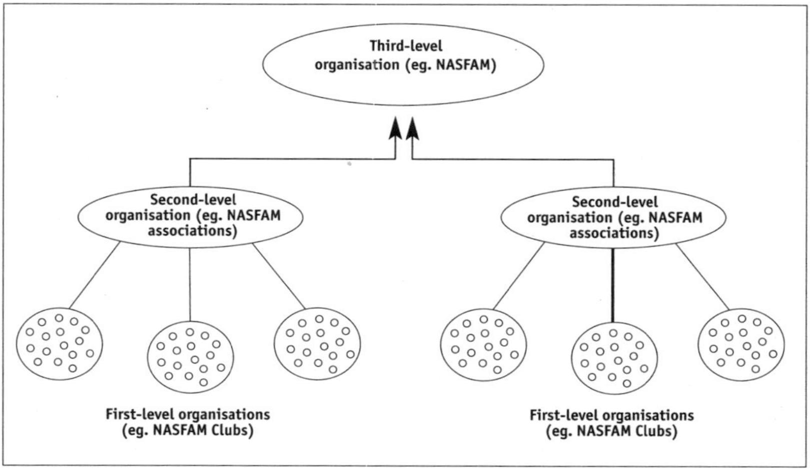

Many POs only have one or two levels of organisation. For example, the Clam Clubs described in Case Study 2 are three independent POs that have not created a second-level organisation. The next case study describes NASFAM, a large PO in Malawi that has developed three levels of organisation.

Case Study 3: NASFAM, Malawi

In 1995, the support organisation ACDI/VOCA began a project aimed at helping existing clubs of small-scale burley tobacco farmers to strengthen their business. Through local support centres the project helped the clubs to improve the quantity and quality of production in order to get higher prices. At the beginning, individual clubs marketed their tobacco on their own, but soon groups of clubs started working together to market their produce in order to lower their transport costs and improve their bargaining position. After a while, some of these groups of clubs decided to establish formal marketing associations (second-level organisations). The project also provided assistance to these associations to develop strong management and accountable leadership.

In 1997, 14 of these associations came together to establish the National Smallholder Farmers' Association of Malawi (NASFAM), a third-level organisation. At this stage, the national project staff of ACDI/VOCA came under the management of NASFAM, while the international staff became advisers to NASFAM's board, but ACDI/VOCA still controlled NASFAM's budget. Over the following years, the project helped to strengthen the governance and management of NASFAM and the associations. All associations had to follow strict financial and governance rules. The executive directors on NASFAM's board are elected by the Annual General Meeting, which is attended by three representatives from each association. Associations receive some funding for managers' salaries but have to cover all other operational costs from membership fees and income from the services they provide to their members.

Although tobacco has been the most important crop for most associations, new associations were formed after 1997, which specialised in other high-value crops such as chilli and coffee. Through economies of scale in marketing and by selling directly to processors or exporters, the associations have been able to get higher prices and increase the profits of producers.

In 2001, the decision was taken to manage the services provided by NASFAM under separate organisations to improve their management. As a result NASFAM has become a holding company, NASFAM Development Corporation (NASDEC), which is owned by the second-level associations. NASDEC owns two subsidiary organisations: NASFAM Commodity Marketing Exchange, a commercial trading company, and NASFAM Centre for Development Support, a non-profit organisation, funded largely by donors, which is responsible for development activities, including policy and advocacy work and developing the capacity of clubs and associations.

As noted above, POs often create additional levels of organisation in order to increase the scale of their business without sacrificing the benefits of small, first-level groups and the ability to co-ordinate and manage the activities of a large number of members. This is one of the main rationales for multi-level POs but it is not the only one. POs also create additional levels of organisation in order to perform specific functions and provide different services to their members. In the case of NASFAM, the third-level organisation was set up by the second-level associations to perform specific functions, including commercial marketing and trading, lobbying, and development activities.

POs often mix different types of legal structure. For example, Agrolempa is a first-level association of farmers that owns a private company (see Figure 6.2).

The purpose of such mixed structures is to take advantage of the main benefits of different types of legal structure and to separate the different functions of the PO. In the case of Agrolempa the members benefit from the simplicity and flexibility of an association to manage their internal affairs while benefiting from the limited liability, credibility, and stronger management structure of a private company when it comes to managing their business. Another important advantage of such structures is that they create a clear separation between the governance of the organisation and the management of the business. This is an important point, which we will return to in the next chapter.

Although the trading company also markets the fruit and vegetables of its members, its main focus is regional trade. The company buys 65 per cent of the fruit and vegetables it trades from producers in other parts of El Salvador and in neighbouring countries to meet supply contracts with many different buyers in El Salvador. Agrolempa is an example of a 'portal company' whose services and business activities reach far beyond the members who own the company.

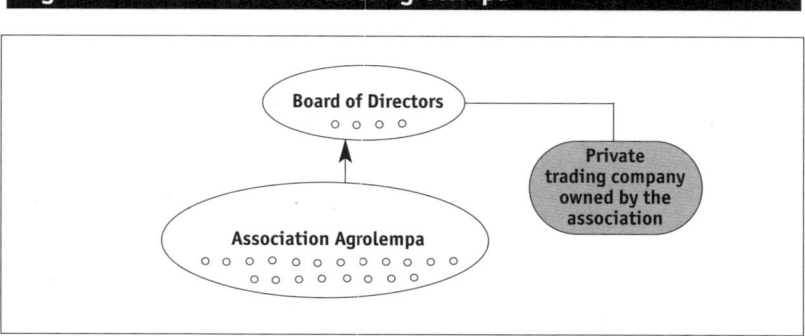

Figure 6. 2: A mixed structure: Agrolempa

Multi-level and mixed structures are often essential for POs to create the necessary scale and management structures in order to compete and increase their bargaining power in the market. However, to manage such structures efficiently and effectively demands considerable skills, experience, and resources. When such structures are not managed effectively there is a real danger that members' ownership, trust, and commitment is weakened, which can sometimes lead to the collapse of the organisation. UCASN, a third-level union of POs in Mozambique (described in Case Study 4 in Chapter 7), provides a good example of the dangers of developing additional levels too quickly and building from the top down.

Summary: PO structure

- There is no 'ideal' legal structure for POs as each of the five types has advantages and disadvantages that need to be considered carefully.
- Multi-level organisations should be developed gradually and organically, according to the needs of the business and the management capacity of the PO's members.
- Mixed PO structures provide a means of combining various benefits of different legal structures.

7 | Producer organisation governance and management

This chapter looks at the internal governance and management of POs, in particular how different POs manage decision-making, what factors affect the governance of POs, and how POs manage business profits. First we will look at another case study of a PO in Mozambique.

Case Study 4: UCASN, Mozambique

The Union of Peasants and Associations of Southern Niassa (UCASN, União de Camponeses e Associações do Sul de Niassa) is an association of small-scale farmers in southern Niassa province in Mozambique. With the support of Oxfam GB and CLUSA (Co-operative League of the USA), the organisation was officially registered as UCASN in 2001. The group started as a small onion-marketing initiative but then got involved in the land-reform process representing the rights of small farmers. Today, UCASN is an agricultural marketing association, responding to the social, cultural, and economic needs of small-scale farmers. The main problems of small farmers in Niassa province are a lack of agricultural service markets, low agricultural productivity, and poor infrastructure, which limits their access to markets. From the start, UCASN has also had to overcome widespread distrust towards collective agricultural initiatives, as a result of the negative historical experiences with co-operatives in Mozambique.

A European-Union-funded support programme enabled UCASN to expand its membership from 65 associations in three districts in 2000 to 254 associations, representing over 7,000 farmers in five districts by 2006. These first-level associations are organised into second-level unions, which are then represented by UCASN, the third-level, apex organisation. UCASN is governed by a Board of Directors elected by the General Assembly, an annual meeting of all the members of the association. The board appoints operational managers who are responsible for all commercial activities, while a Fiscal Oversight Committee provides additional monitoring and control of the union's finances.

> UCASN promotes access to high-value markets and negotiates advance contracts with companies for products such as white sesame and soya. These companies often provide seeds and the association gets higher prices by cutting out informal traders. Some associations also try to market maize but they have had difficulties competing with informal traders who are very efficient and operate with low margins.
>
> As a result of rapid growth of the Union from 2000, with the creation of new associations and second-level unions, some grassroots members do not have a strong sense of ownership of the organisation. Another factor has been frequent delays in payments to members and the lack of a clear payment system that is understood by all members. Oxfam GB is supporting UCASN with the development of a new strategic plan, which will seek to address some of these problems. Despite these challenges, UCASN has enabled many of its members to access higher value markets and has made some progress in recent years towards financial sustainability.

Decision-making structures and systems

In new or small POs all members are usually involved in managing the business and making day-to-day decisions. However, as POs grow and the number of members increases, it is not practical for every member to be involved in decision-making. There is a need for some form of delegation, i.e. choosing representatives to manage the PO on behalf of the members. UCASN, like most POs, is governed with the following two-level structure:

1. The first level is made up of all the PO's members. Their power lies in the decisions made at the general meeting. In most POs, this general meeting involves all members and occurs at least once a year, and is therefore often called the Annual General Meeting (AGM). Decision-making at the AGM is usually conducted by vote: in the case of UCASN as with most associations and all traditional co-operatives, each member has an equal vote; in private companies and hybrid structures, voting is often proportional to each member's investment in the business. At the AGM members elect their leaders, decide what to do with the PO's profits, and agree on major issues, such as new business plans or investment projects.

2. The second level is made up of the leaders elected at the AGM. These leaders or 'directors' are normally elected for a limited term, such as two years, and together they form a management group, which is often called the board of directors. In multi-level POs, each group elects its own leaders to represent it at the next level. The main purpose of the board is to provide leadership and to govern the PO's affairs. In some cases, PO boards may also invite external people to

work with and advise the board. NASFAM's board, for example, involves business and marketing experts who advise the board but do not have voting rights. POs often have additional committees made up of leaders and members, such as UCASN's Financial Oversight Committee, that monitor the activities of the board.

As in many POs, UCASN's board does not actually manage the PO's business on a day-to-day basis. Instead the board has appointed full-time managers, as employees of the PO, to manage the business and report back to the board on a regular basis (see Figure 7.1). There are three main reasons why POs hire professional managers who are not members:

- As POs grow it becomes increasingly difficult for elected leaders to govern the PO, manage the business, *and* have time to manage their own private production.
- The members of a PO often have insufficient business and management skills and experience to manage the business effectively.
- Managing a business in a dynamic market requires quick decisions and a rapid response to changing conditions and new opportunities in the market. However, committees of elected leaders tend to be slow and bureaucratic and professional managers with delegated independence can often manage the business more effectively.

In the case of Agrolempa, the professional managers work in a separate legal structure, the private trading company owned by the association. Although there are good reasons for hiring professional managers it can also create problems: POs often hire managers because none of the members, including the elected leaders, have the necessary management skills and experience – none of Agrolempa's members had the necessary marketing skills to access demanding urban markets. But in this case it can be difficult for elected leaders to monitor the work of the professional

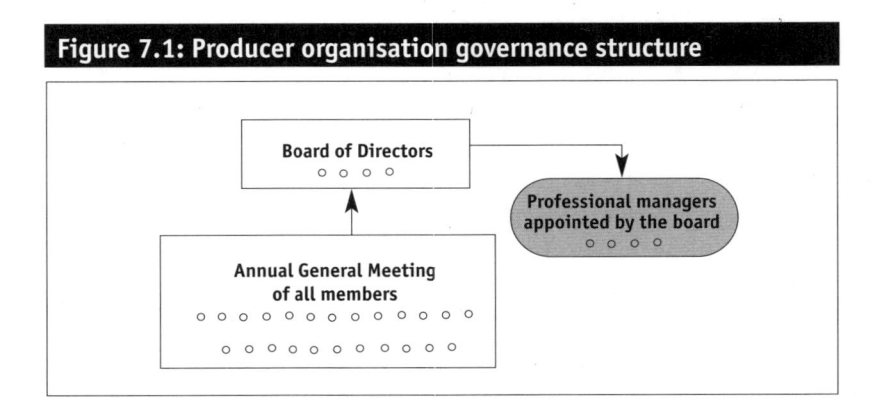

Figure 7.1: Producer organisation governance structure

managers and make sure they do their job properly. This is a problem because managers, whether they are members or hired professionals, can potentially use their position to promote their own interests or even divert PO resources into their own pockets. Members and leaders who do not have the time or understanding to monitor the activities of managers, in particular women or less powerful members, can therefore be cheated by their own organisation. The professional managers working for Agrolempa have a strong commitment to the objectives of the association and so the leaders trust that the managers are acting in their interest. This approach relies on trust and the goodwill of individuals and is therefore not a long-term solution to the problem. In the long term, PO leaders have to develop a reasonable understanding of the business so they can effectively monitor and control the work of hired managers. This can be a particular problem for women as they may struggle to find the time to develop this understanding and may therefore be disadvantaged within the PO. In the case of COMUCAP, members' attitude towards men has been challenged with the hiring of their first male manager, while the manager has also had to change his attitude towards women as employers.

Grassroots ownership

A strong sense of ownership and trust of the leadership among grassroots members is critical for POs to function effectively. When this is missing, POs face real difficulties. For example, although UFP, the Union of Fruit Producers in West Africa, has a formal governance structure that gives members the ability to participate in decision-making, it has faced considerable difficulties in recent years because some grassroots members have lost trust in their elected leaders and no longer felt that the PO was serving their interests. As a result some members left their associations or refused to pay their membership fees. The experience of UFP and some of the other POs described in our case studies provides useful insights into some common governance and management challenges that POs face as they expand and develop:

- *Independent initiative:* some of UFP's first- and second-level associations were established very quickly under a donor-funded programme managed by Oxfam GB. Although the new organisations responded to real problems producers faced in the market, the new associations were driven primarily by external initiative and as a result some members saw the PO as a means of accessing external support rather than as their own initiative. While many POs are established with external involvement, what is important is that, in some way, the PO is the idea of the producers and they see it as their effort to address their problems in the market rather than as someone else's solution to their problem.

- *Organic growth:* as we noted in the last chapter, POs need to develop organically, according to the evolving needs and capacity of their members. For example, NASFAM's second-level associations were created by the initiative of groups of first-level clubs, as they recognised the need to co-operate in order to lower their costs. In the case of UCASN, some of the second-level unions were established under an external support programme at the same time as the first-level associations were being set up. As a result, some of these associations did not develop a strong sense of ownership over their union, which has contributed to a lack of trust and poor communication within the PO.

- *Trust in the leadership:* whatever system of governance is used, POs can only function effectively if their members trust and have confidence in their leaders. A common problem in many POs is that although the constitution may only allow leaders a two- or three-year term in office, leaders often remain in their position for much longer. For example, in UFP, a small group of producers from one area who originally set up the PO continue to control the overall leadership of the PO many years later. As a result grassroots members from other areas have become increasingly suspicious of the leaders, leading to internal tensions that have weakened the PO's business. In the case of UCASN, poor communication between the different levels of the PO was made worse by the fact that many members did not understand the PO's payment system. As a result, members were often uncertain whether the PO was really paying them a fair price.

- *Grassroots capacity:* as the last example highlighted, unless grassroots members have the necessary understanding of the PO and its business, it is difficult for them to participate in decision-making or to know whether the PO is really serving their interests. AGMs can be a bureaucratic process in which members merely approve the proposals put forward by the leadership. This is not surprising as most POs reflect the existing power and gender relations within the community. It can be very difficult for individual members and women in particular to challenge these power relations, especially when elections are conducted with a show of hands rather than through a secret ballot. Good governance and management within POs therefore also depends on individual members having the capacity, confidence, and freedom to participate in decision-making. For example, women were largely excluded from membership and decision-making in Fedecares, a federation of small-scale coffee producer associations in the Dominican Republic. Changes to the PO's rules (giving membership to the whole family rather than just to individuals) *and* significant investments to develop the capacity of women to participate in decision-making (through leadership training and organising separate meetings for women) were necessary in order to increase women's participation at all levels of the PO. In Mozambique, CLUSA have tried to address this problem by providing literacy and numeracy training to women in order to increase their confidence and ability to participate in the PO's affairs.

Managing profits

For many POs, deciding what to do with business profits is a difficult task. This is because there is often a conflict between the short-term interests of members and the long-term sustainability of the business. For example, a coffee co-operative in Central America had a confrontation between the members and the leaders: the members wanted the co-operative to pay out all the profits to them as their rightful 'dividend' on their share of the business; the leaders, however, were thinking about the long-term needs of the business and they proposed to withhold most of the profits to increase the PO's working capital. This is a common struggle within POs and it is often most acute during the early years of development, when members have limited understanding of the PO's business, or when there is a lack of trust and confidence in the leadership.

This tension is particularly challenging because many POs face difficulties raising money for investments. Even though Agrolempa is now a recognised trading company in El Salvador, so far it has not been able to access competitive financing from commercial banks because of the nature of its business, working with small-scale agricultural producers. As the members of most POs have very limited assets, POs cannot usually turn to their owners for investment and so trading profits often represent the only source of investment capital.

This difficulty highlights the importance of the system of ownership and the principle used to allocate profits. POs tend to distribute profits to members based on one of the following two principles:

1. Profits are distributed according to members' share of ownership, i.e. how much money each member has invested in the business. For example, the Clam Clubs in Viet Nam distributed the profits to each member according to how much they had invested in clam production at the beginning of the season.

2. Profits are distributed based on patronage, i.e. how much each member has sold or bought through the PO. In UCASN, for example, profits are distributed according to the value of produce each member has sold to their association.

These principles affect members' incentives and motivation to invest in the PO or use the PO's services, so the choice of principle is important. The members of the Clam Clubs, for example, have a strong motivation to invest in clam-raising because the more money they invest, the bigger their share of profits. In contrast, the members of UCASN have much less incentive to invest in the business because profits will not be distributed according to how much they have invested, and when they want to retire they cannot sell their share of the business because shares are not tradable. Of course, even when there is a strong incentive to invest in the business, many small-scale producers do not have the resources to take advantage of such opportunities and so only wealthier members benefit. This is why a special revolving fund was set up for poorer members of the Clam Clubs, enabling them to borrow funds to invest in the business.

Summary: PO governance and management

- POs can be governed in many different ways and there is no single, 'best' approach.
- The challenge all POs face is to adapt governance structures and systems to the capacity and needs of members, the demands of the business, and their stage of development.
- Grassroots ownership and trust in the leadership is essential for POs' survival. This depends on the PO being driven by producers' own initiative, the organic growth of the PO, transparent leadership, and grassroots capacity to participate in decision-making.
- POs can manage business profits in different ways but it is important that they develop a system that satisfies members without weakening the business.

8 | Producer organisation business strategies

As we noted in the introduction to this guide, in the past, many agencies working with producers and POs focused their attention on increasing the productivity of producers and raising the total output of POs, with little attention to market demand. In today's markets, no PO will survive for long without first identifying what consumers and buyers want and organising all its activities, including individual production and collective services, to meet these needs.

To compete in the market *and* deliver real benefits to their members in the long term, POs have to make a profit, sooner or later, and therefore they must continually find ways of increasing their income and decreasing their costs. Each service POs provide to their members involves costs and unless it can provide these services at lower cost than other businesses in the market, the PO's business will fail because its members will be able to access the same services at better prices elsewhere. For example, a PO in Southern Africa recently went bankrupt because it was not able to operate its processing and trading services at a profit *and* still pay its members attractive prices. One way POs can reduce their costs and minimise the risk of failure is to outsource as many services as possible. The coffee co-operative Gumatindu in Uganda, for example, has subcontracted most of its processing and marketing activities to independent service providers, while maintaining ownership of its coffee. POs sometimes try to provide services to their members that no one else is offering, but there is often a reason why these services are not provided by the private sector: in many cases they are simply not profitable because they involve high transaction costs and risks for individual traders. Unless a PO manages to reduce these transaction costs, for example by taking advantage of economies of scale, it is unlikely to succeed where other businesses have failed. In Mozambique, for example, a large PO tried to compete with informal traders in the local maize market. Although the PO managed to cut out the traders who came to the farm gate and paid low prices, the PO was unable to compete with traders in the district wholesale market, as the traders' experience and networks enabled them to operate at lower cost than the PO.

These examples show how important it is for PO services to be based on a careful analysis of the market and the real costs of doing business. Below we will look at the most common business strategies adopted by POs to raise their profits, either by increasing their business income or by lowering their costs. We will then consider how POs increase their bargaining power and lower their risks. First we will introduce another case study of a group of co-operatives in Palestine.

Case Study 5: Olive-Oil Co-operatives, Palestine

Palestinian farmers have cultivated olives for many centuries. In the 1960s many olive-oil co-operatives were established in the West Bank, and Palestinian olive oil was exported to many Arab countries. However, olive-oil production and export suffered heavily as a result of the occupation and uprisings in the following decades, and Palestinian olive oil lost its position in these markets. Since 2000, a number of Palestinian and international NGOs have begun to revitalise many of the old co-operatives and promote export production. Palestinian olives can produce high-quality olive oil, and as the production and marketing costs in Palestine are relatively high, the best strategy is to improve the quality of the olive oil and target high-value markets in the West rather than compete in local markets, where volume is more important than quality.

The Palestinian Farmers Union (PFU) has been working with a number of old co-operatives but has often found it easier to develop new co-operatives out of informal groups than to revive the old structures. The opportunity of accessing export markets has encouraged co-operation and unless farmers work together they are unable to gather enough olives to operate the oil presses on a daily basis. Daily pressing is critical to ensure the olive oil meets the required quality standards. Accessing European markets also requires the producers to meet very demanding traceability and certification requirements, which individual farmers cannot afford. These incentives have encouraged the small-scale producers to unite and change their practices despite their initial doubts about co-operation.

The co-operatives supported by PFU, Oxfam GB, and other support organisations have a traditional co-operative structure, with a board of directors elected by the general assembly and operational managers appointed by the board. Within the co-operatives, traditional leaders often control decision-making and, so far, marginalised members of the community, especially women, have limited influence. An important focus of PFU's work with the co-operatives is to develop a second-level organisation which can promote and defend the interests of small-scale producers in the Palestinian

> Olive Oil Council which has been dominated by commercial producers and processing companies. There is also a plan to establish a producer-owned olive-oil bottling and marketing company, which will enable small-scale producers to develop their own brand and control more of the market chain.

Increasing business income

POs adopt many different strategies to increase their income, including increasing the volume of sales or adding value to their produce, and POs often combine these strategies to achieve their business aims. Of course, increased bargaining power also enables POs to increase their income but we will deal with this point separately, below.

Raising volume

A basic strategy for POs to increase their business income is to increase the volume of sales, i.e. to produce and sell more of the same product. One market option for the Palestinian olive-oil co-operatives was to enter the domestic olive-oil market. This market deals with low-quality oil that is traded at low prices and so producers have to sell large quantities to make a profit. The co-operatives realised that it would be difficult for them to compete with large commercial farms that could produce large quantities at much lower cost and so they turned their attention to the export market where competition is based on quality. This situation is not unique as POs often find it difficult, if not impossible, to compete in low-value markets where competition is based on driving down costs. Even if a PO can successfully increase volumes without increasing their costs, the low profit margins will rarely generate attractive incomes for individual members.

Adding value

Adding value can involve three different strategies: improving quality, processing, or differentiation:

- *Improving quality:* another strategy to increase income is to obtain higher prices by improving the quality of an existing product. Agrolempa, for example, has been able to obtain higher prices by improving the quality of its members' fruit and vegetable production and targeting markets that pay a premium for good quality. Quality improvements can involve relatively simple investments in sorting, grading, or cleaning a product or more costly investments in better inputs and production equipment and improved storage and handling facilities. NASFAM, for example, has had to invest in an internal quality-control system to ensure that the groundnuts it exports to Europe meet strict European Union food-safety standards, while

OAPI, a PO in India (see Case Study 7), has succeeded in obtaining organic certification, which enables its farmers to receive a premium for their cotton.

- *Processing:* by processing a product a PO can increase its value and deal directly with buyers of the processed product. Although processing may seem like a straightforward way for POs to obtain higher prices, in practice, processing requires significant resources and management experience, which most POs only develop after many years in business and often with significant external support.
Case Study 6 provides a good example of this strategy. POs either own processing equipment themselves, as in the case of Zadrima, or they sub-contract processing to an independent processor. OAPI, for example (Case Study 7), will pay to have its members' seed cotton processed at an independent local ginnery (the cotton-processing factory) as this is a lot cheaper and less risky than trying to invest in their own processing plant. In this way the farmers have cut out intermediary traders who pay low prices and receive a share of the value added to the seed cotton through processing.

- *Differentiation:* to compete in high-value speciality markets, POs need to give their products a unique identity, which differentiates their product from others in the market. Few POs have the resources and capacity to develop a successful brand in their local market, let alone for an export market, but when it is successful this strategy allows producers to receive a share in much higher retail prices. For example, the Zadrima co-operative in Albania is trying to build a recognised brand name for its wine in the local market. For this strategy to succeed, the co-operative has to invest heavily in production and processing, to improve the quality and consistency of its wine, and in publicity to increase awareness of its brand among local consumers and buyers. In St Lucia, four co-operatives have jointly invested in a shared brand for local fresh horticultural produce, to differentiate their goods in the local hotel and supermarket sector from US imports.

Diversification into high-value products

All the business strategies so far involve using an existing product and adding value to it. In some cases, small-scale producers may however produce low-value products for which there are no higher value markets. For example, in north Mozambique, there are few markets that pay a premium for higher quality maize and most people prefer to mill their maize at home, so the market for maize flour is also limited. In this context, the only option for UCASN was to encourage its members to diversify production into high-quality products, such as chilli peppers or

Case Study 6: Zadrima Co-operative, Albania

Grapes have been cultivated in the Shkoder area of northern Albania for centuries, but the vineyards were neglected in the agricultural policies of the socialist era. Since the transition to a market economy began in the early 1990s, many farmers have struggled to make a living. The old vineyards in Shkoder did not receive much attention as they required significant investment and many of the skills had been lost. However, some of the younger men in the village worked on vineyards in Italy as labour migrants and when they returned they persuaded others in the village to gather the grapes from their individual vineyards and produce wine together.

In 2003, a group of ten farmers from Shkoder asked Oxfam GB to help with purchasing basic wine-making equipment and rehabilitating their cantina, the building where the wine is produced. Oxfam GB agreed and also provided training for the group, in business and organisational management, and paid for a wine specialist to help the producers improve the production process. The group was formally registered in 2003 as the Zadrima association and received further grants from Oxfam GB in the following years for vineyard equipment and storage tanks. The tanks were an important investment as they enabled the PO to access more valuable markets by improving the quality and consistency of the wine.

At the beginning the members of the group produced their wine separately and sold it in recycled plastic bottles to local cafes. Following the investment in improved production equipment the group took the important step to combine their grapes and produce and market their wine collectively. The association now began marketing their wine in improved plastic containers with a simple label. In 2005, the group sold their wine for the first time in proper glass bottles with a good-quality label at a national trade fair.

In the same year the association decided it was time to register their business as a co-operative, to establish itself as a proper business structure and to improve its credibility. Although the co-operative has made significant progress over the last few years, it is operating in a very competitive market and is also facing internal challenges. The most important factor that determines the quality of the wine is the quality of the grapes and this can create tensions because not all members of the co-operative make the same effort in production and some produce better quality grapes than others. However, all members receive the same price for their grapes and so there is little incentive for individual members to invest their own money and effort in improving the quality of grapes. The co-operative will have to develop a way to reward and therefore encourage investments in quality or it will not be able to compete in the national market in the long term.

sesame seed. Producers of traditional commodities such as coffee or cocoa may face similar problems unless they can add value to their product through differentiation. High-value products can provide good income but to access these markets POs have to make considerable investments to produce the quantity, quality, and consistency required by buyers.

Market development

POs can also increase their income by influencing the perceptions and attitudes of buyers and consumers and thereby increasing the demand for their produce. For example, the four co-operatives in St Lucia mentioned above have encouraged consumers to buy locally produced fruit and vegetables sold through national supermarkets. With the help of Oxfam GB the co-operatives have also succeeded in changing perceptions within the hotel sector towards local producers. As a result the co-operatives have negotiated long-term supply contracts with a number of hotels that represent a valuable new market for producers while also lowering the hotels' procurement costs.

Lowering business costs

Finding ways to lower business costs is just as important for POs' ability to compete in the market although POs often focus a lot of attention on ways to access higher prices. There are many ways POs can lower their costs and we consider a few in more detail below.

Scale economies

In Chapter 3 we highlighted the importance of economies of scale in helping POs to lower their costs. Most of the POs in our case studies have lowered each member's marketing costs considerably by bulking their produce and marketing it collectively. These economies of scale provide immediate benefits for members but to compete with large commercial producers POs will often have to find additional ways of lowering their costs. NASFAM, for example, is providing inputs at lower costs to its members by purchasing seeds and fertilisers in bulk. By managing processing more carefully, the co-operatives in Palestine have been able to lower their processing costs while also improving the quality of the olive oil. POs can also achieve important scale economies in accessing market services, such as market information, extension, or transport services.

Lowering internal transaction costs

POs have to conduct many internal transactions within the organisation to supply inputs or collect and market members' produce. In multi-level POs these transactions can be complex as produce has to be collected and stored in first-level associations, then transported to a second-level association, where larger quantities are stored, before being delivered to the buyer. If this system is not managed effectively and efficiently the internal transaction costs can rise, leading to additional transport and storage costs, lost income as produce cannot be delivered on time, and production problems if inputs are supplied late. Many POs also face problems because of poorly managed financial systems or delays in payment from buyers. In Ghana, the co-operative Kuapa Kokoo faced a major financial crisis because it took around three months to collect cocoa from producers and sell it on to buyers. This meant that the co-operative had to borrow money for this period, which placed a heavy burden on its business. By introducing a new deferred payment system and improving staff transport the co-operative no longer had to borrow money and members only had to wait for about two weeks before receiving payment.

Increased bargaining power

As underlined in Part I, increased bargaining power is an important benefit and rationale of POs. Increased bargaining power can enable producers to negotiate higher prices for their produce, lower input prices, and gain better terms for their transaction. In Chapter 10, we will also look at how POs can influence the market environment to defend and promote their interests. Here we look at three strategies POs adopt to increase their bargaining power in the market.

- *Scarcity value:* producers tend to have some bargaining power when they sell a product that is scarce, i.e. in short supply. If a PO focuses on marketing a product that is in short supply (and therefore has 'scarcity value') they are likely to enjoy a much better bargaining position than for products which are plentiful in the market. However, this often only applies to products that have certain characteristics or are supplied in a certain way. For example, Agrolempa has been able to negotiate good prices by supplying the quality and quantity of fruit and vegetables preferred by certain buyers.
- *Restructuring trading arrangements:* another strategy to increase bargaining power is for producers to restructure their trading arrangements so that they bypass exploitative traders. The case of OAPI (Case Study 7) provides an example of this approach. To access higher value and more competitive markets for their cotton, the co-operatives have had to take control of the next stage in the cotton-market chain, i.e. processing the cotton. To save costs and reduce risks, OAPI will contract a ginnery to process their members' cotton before selling the processed cotton to buyers further down the chain. This practice, where a company controls a product at more than one stage in the market chain, is called vertical integration.

- *Market power:* a further strategy to increase bargaining power is to control a significant share of trade in a particular market so that buyers are forced to do business with you. For example, Asprepatía, an association of panela producers in Colombia (see Case Study 8), buys a large share of all the panela produced in the Patía region and it can therefore influence the market price for panela. Informal traders now have to offer the same price as Asprepatía if they want to buy from small-scale producers (see Figure 8.1). Although this strategy has been very successful in the case of Asprepatía, it only works in specific circumstances, i.e. when traders are actually exploiting producers and market channels can be controlled by a single large PO. As noted above, UCASN was unable to displace traders in the local maize market, as UCASN was unable to control a significant share of the market.

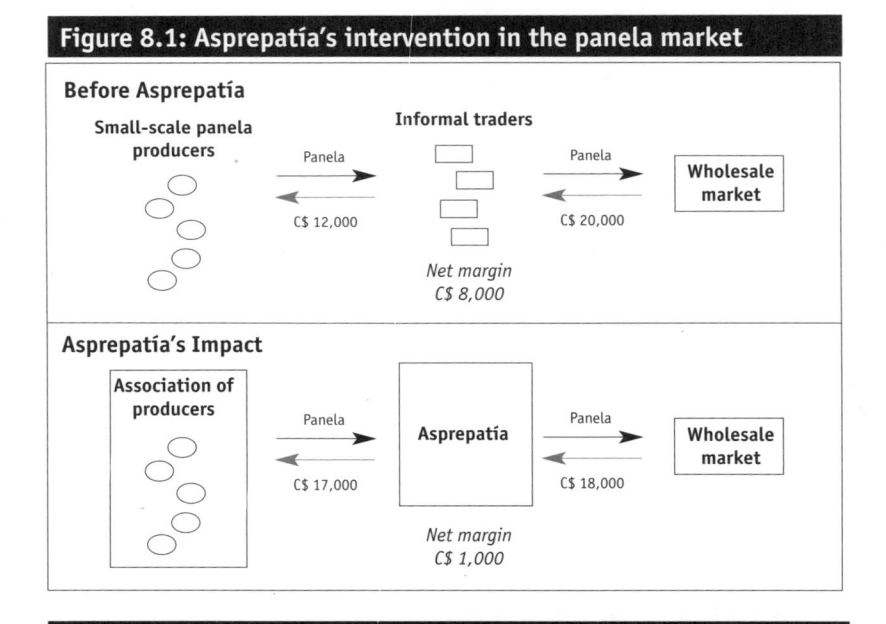

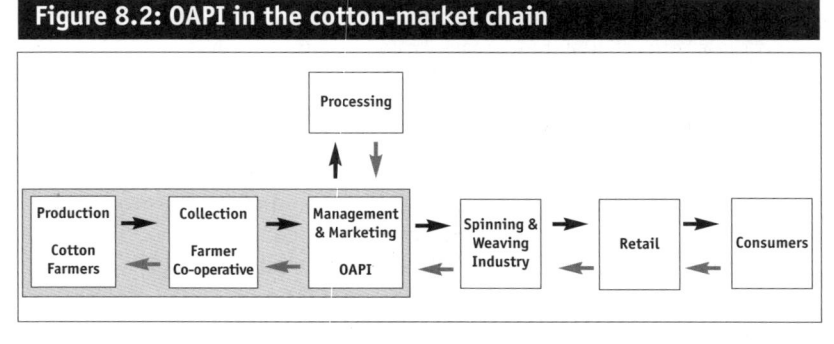

Figure 8.1: Asprepatía's intervention in the panela market

Before Asprepatía

Small-scale panela producers → Panela C$ 12,000 → Informal traders → Panela C$ 20,000 → Wholesale market

Net margin C$ 8,000

Asprepatía's Impact

Association of producers → Panela C$ 17,000 → Asprepatía → Panela C$ 18,000 → Wholesale market

Net margin C$ 1,000

Figure 8.2: OAPI in the cotton-market chain

Production / Cotton Farmers → Collection / Farmer Co-operative → Management & Marketing / OAPI ↔ Processing

Management & Marketing / OAPI → Spinning & Weaving Industry → Retail → Consumers

60 | Producer Organisations: A Guide to Developing Collective Rural Enterprises

Case Study 7: Oorvi Agricultural Products India (OAPI), Private Ltd.

Over the last decade, small-scale cotton farmers in India have been hit hard by economic liberalisation, which has led to rising costs of production and cheap cotton imports. Small-scale farmers usually have very little bargaining power and have faced growing exploitation from buyers and input suppliers. The intensive use of agro-chemicals has led to a fall in production levels as soil quality has deteriorated. The result has been a sharp increase in rural poverty and a disturbing number of cases of suicide of destitute farmers who have lost hope.

To compete in the cotton market and create more sustainable farming practices, four farmer co-operatives, supported by Oxfam GB and other organisations, have switched to organic cotton production using locally available inputs. This has reduced their cost of production by up to 60 per cent and will enable members to obtain a premium for organic cotton. To address farmers' weak position in the local cotton market, the co-operatives supported the creation of a private trading company, OAPI, in 2006, that will buy seed cotton from small-scale farmers through existing and new farmer co-operatives. The company will sub-contract the ginning process to an independent processing company and then sell the processed cotton to the weaving industry (see Figure 8.1). In this way farmers will control the processing stage and will be able to receive a share of the higher price of processed cotton.

Although the aim is for the farmers to own and control the company, the existing co-operatives have not yet developed the capacity to control and manage the company effectively. There were also concerns that stronger members would dominate the company and that the interests of new or weaker members would be ignored. It would have taken a number of years for the co-operative to develop the necessary management capacity but urgent action is needed to improve the position of small-scale cotton farmers and prevent further destitution. Oxfam GB therefore decided to finance the business and, initially, will be the largest shareholder. The plan is for Oxfam GB gradually to transfer all its shares to the farmer co-operatives over the coming years.

OAPI is registered as a private limited company as the nature of the cotton business demands a structure that can respond quickly to a dynamic market and changing financial needs. The private limited company structure also provides a better control framework for Oxfam GB, who, as the majority shareholder, can ensure skilled and knowledgeable managers are employed to manage the business until the co-operatives have developed the necessary capacity to run the trading company. See Figure 8.2 which shows how OAPI fits into the market chain.

Lowering market risks

Diversification is an important strategy POs adopt to lower their business risks and guarantee a stable income. Although product diversification can reduce market risk, market diversification, i.e. producing the same product for different markets, is often an easier and more effective strategy. For example, rather than focusing on export markets, Agrolempa has tried to access a range of markets, including long-term contracts with government departments, less secure contracts with supermarkets, and other supply agreements with restaurants and wholesale markets. This spread or mixture of contracts has reduced the risk and uncertainty of the business and enabled Agrolempa to invest in the business and plan for the future.

Another factor that affects risk is the nature of the market linkages, i.e. relationships between POs and buyers. In the past most products were sold in so-called spot markets, where buyers and sellers negotiate and complete a transaction 'on the spot', i.e. right away. For example, the Clam Clubs in Viet Nam sell their clams to whichever trader offers the best price on the day. In today's buyer-driven markets, more and more sales are made through longer-term contracts between producers and buyers. For example, Agrolempa has negotiated long-term supply contracts with both government departments (e.g. hospitals and prisons) and supermarkets.

Many buyers prefer advance or 'forward contracts' because it enables them to reduce their risks and meet the demands of retailers. UCASN, for example, works with export companies that make supply contracts for paprika with its unions. The company provides the farmers with paprika seeds and some training and then deducts the cost of the seeds from the final payment to the producers at harvest time. Table 8.1 identifies some of the main advantages and disadvantages of spot markets and contractual arrangements for POs.

Table 8.1: Advantages and disadvantages of different types of market linkages

	'Spot' markets	Contractual arrangements
Advantages for POs	There is no obligation to sell products to any particular buyer. POs are free to find the best offer for each transaction.	The business risk is shared between producers and buyers. Producers can have a secure and stable income if the relationship is fair and transparent. Buyers may provide additional market services, which producers cannot obtain in the market.
Disadvantages for POs	PO members take on all the business risk. Prices and income are uncertain and it can be difficult to plan production and investments if income from sales is unpredictable.	POs have to stick to the contract even if they would be able to receive better terms or prices from other buyers. If individual members or associations break the contract ('side-selling') the whole PO may lose future business.

Summary: PO business strategies

- POs can only survive in the long term if they make a profit by continually raising their income or lowering their costs.
- There is no ideal business strategy for POs, as each PO has to find a combination of strategies that fits the capacity of the PO, its objectives, and, most importantly, the markets it is trying to access.
- While some strategies, such as processing or diversifying into high-value products, can increase POs' income considerably, they often require considerable skills, experience, and resources that many POs only acquire after many years of business.
- Although size is important, increased bargaining power often depends on other factors, such as the ability to produce scarce products that meet buyers' preferences.
- POs can reduce market risks by diversifying into different markets or products or by entering long-term contractual arrangements with buyers, providing they can negotiate a fair deal.

9 | Producer organisation access to market services

To conduct their trade and develop their business, POs, like any other business, need to access different types of market services. These market services are illustrated in Figure 9.1, and fall into two main categories:

1. Market services that are required by any type of business in order to conduct their trade, e.g. production, financial, market information, or transport services.
2. Market services aimed at developing the general capacity of the PO, e.g. organisational development or management training.

Figure 9.1: Market services required by producer organisations

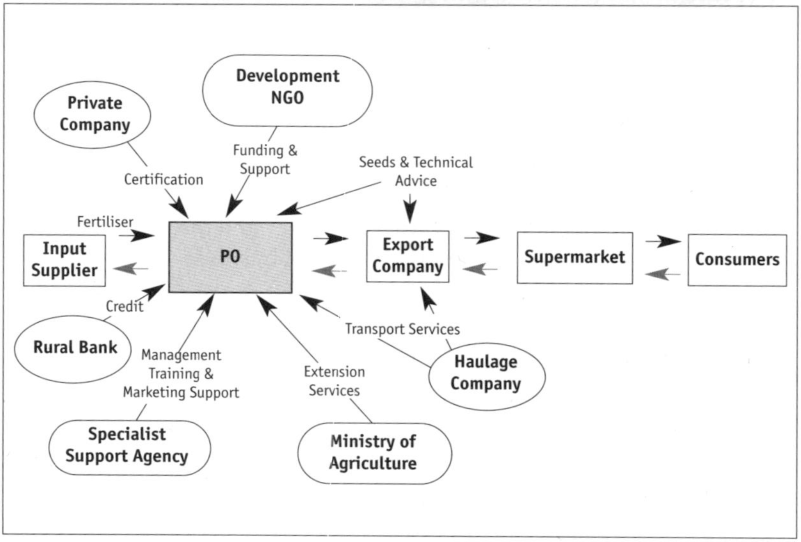

As suggested in Figure 9.1, these services can be provided by many different kinds of organisations, including commercial companies, specialist agencies, development NGOs, government agencies, and POs themselves. There are six main ways in which these market services are provided:

1. *Embedded market services:* embedded services are market services that are provided as part of another business transaction and are therefore embedded within that transaction. For example, UCASN association receive paprika seeds on credit as part of their supply contract with the export company.

2. *Independent commercial market services:* many market services are provided by independent commercial service providers. For example, transport and financial services are provided independently by commercial companies and financial institutions. NGOs and specialist support agencies can often play a useful role linking POs to independent service providers. In Mozambique, for example, CLUSA negotiated a service agreement between a rural bank and a PO for the bank to offer small loans to the PO's members.

3. *Government market services:* government ministries sometimes provide important market services, such as extension training for farmers and market information services. Many developing-country governments that want to promote POs need to play a critical role in supporting the provision of market services. Asprepatía, for example (Case Study 8), received support from a state vocational training college to develop the skills of its members.

4. *Externally funded, non-commercial market services:* specialist support agencies, such as ACDI/VOCA which worked with NASFAM, or development NGOs, provide market services to POs with funds from donors or private donations. These organisations often provide substantial grant funding to help POs set up their business and invest in capital assets. In Part III we will take a closer look at the role of development NGOs in providing these services.

5. *PO services:* sometimes POs decide to operate their own market services for the organisation and its members. For example, Agrolempa provides extension services to its members and NASFAM has set up its own farm supply shops where members can purchase inputs on credit. In Mozambique, a large PO supported by CLUSA has recently set up Business and Support Services Centres known as CAN (Centros de Apoio e de Negócios) under a small group of second-level associations. The CAN are responsible for quality control, raising productivity through extension to increase volumes and achieve economies of scale, input supply, and providing access to information

and technology. At present the centres' costs are part-funded by CLUSA but the aim is for second-level associations to cover their costs in full.

6. *PO networks:* sometimes a group of POs may come together to form a network to mobilise resources and provide market services to member POs. For example, in Ghana a group of POs have set up a network called MAPRONET with the support of Oxfam GB and other facilitating agencies. MAPRONET provides market services to its 46 member associations, including helping them to attend trade fairs to meet buyers, and business and management training.

In many remote and thin rural markets, essential market services are not provided in any way, or are only provided at a very high cost that POs cannot afford. Private market service providers are unwilling to invest in the provision of these services as the costs and risks of business are too high. However, without these services the market cannot develop and so the costs and risks of doing business remain high. State intervention is therefore often necessary either to provide essential market services directly to producers or to offer incentives to private market service providers. In the next chapter we will consider the important role POs can play in lobbying the government for such interventions.

As the above examples have highlighted, many POs rely on external support and funding to access the market services they require to conduct and develop their business. While such support is essential to create a more level playing field for small-scale producers, especially in their early stage of development, in the long term POs need to find financially sustainable ways of accessing essential market services that are not dependent on external grants. This presents a particular challenge for development NGOs supporting POs and we will return to this issue in Part III.

Summary: PO access to market services

- POs depend on market services to conduct and develop their business effectively.
- Market services are provided in many different ways and by a wide range of agencies, including individuals, private companies, government agencies, and NGOs.
- A significant challenge for POs in the long term is to find financially sustainable ways of accessing these market services.

10 | Influencing the market environment

In Chapter 2 we noted that small-scale producers often have little influence on the market itself or on the wider economic, political, and natural environment that affects the market and therefore their livelihoods. National and international market and trade policies frequently ignore the needs and interests of small-scale producers and continue to prioritise the interests of either a small political elite, large commercial producers and investors, or a minority of 'high potential' small-scale producers. For example, although small-scale producers make up the majority of the population in Mozambique, their geographical isolation and lack of organisation means that their interests are often overlooked in the land-reform process. While large private companies can mobilise considerable resources to persuade regional governments to allocate communal land for private business investments, small-scale producers' rights to the land are often ignored. Land rights are an important issue in the 'market environment' that affects the markets and livelihood of producers, but there are many other institutions, laws, policies, norms, and resources that affect the market. Figure 10.1 illustrates some of the main factors that make up the market environment.

Although our definition of POs in Part I emphasises their role as rural businesses, businesses can only survive in a market environment that:

1. contributes to a more level playing field and creates equal opportunities for small-scale producers, and
2. facilitates non-discriminatory, efficient, and effective market exchanges.

As we noted in Chapter 2, liberalised and buyer-driven markets often do not constitute an environment in which small-scale producers can compete on an equal basis alongside large companies and commercial farms. Furthermore, rural markets are often biased against small-scale producers, especially women, and are neither efficient nor effective.

Figure 10.1: The market environment

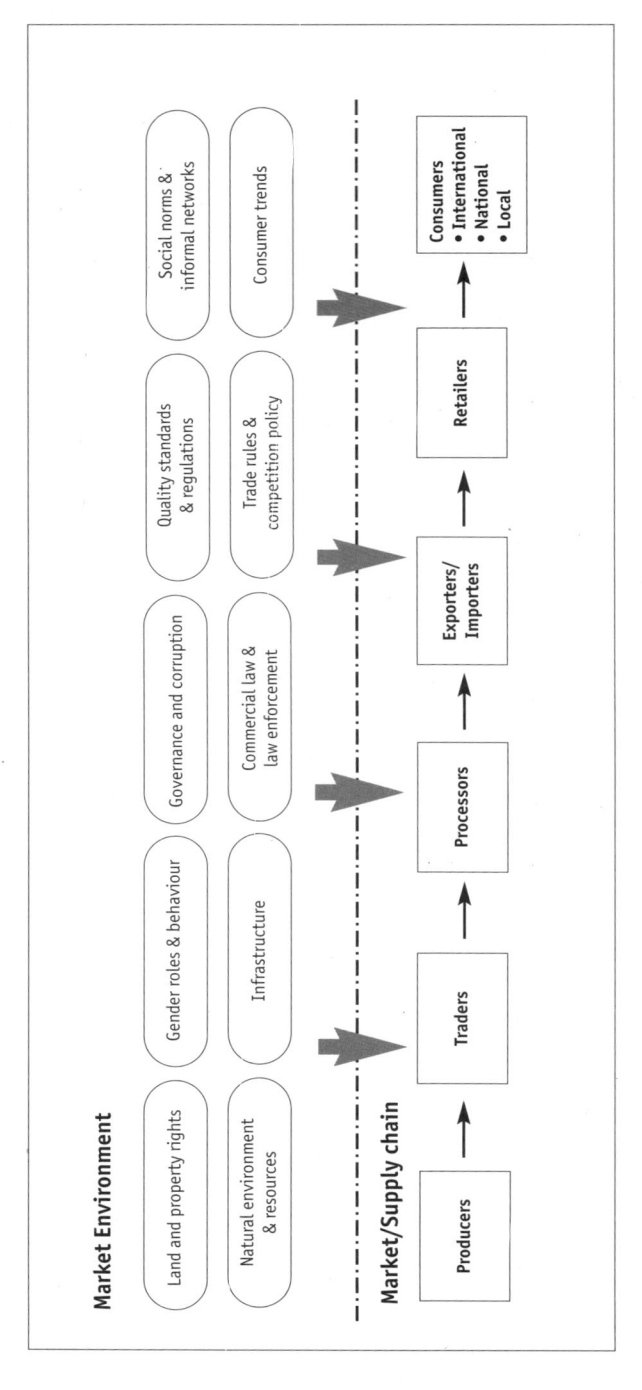

Market Environment

- Land and property rights
- Gender roles & behaviour
- Governance and corruption
- Quality standards & regulations
- Social norms & informal networks
- Natural environment & resources
- Infrastructure
- Commercial law & law enforcement
- Trade rules & competition policy
- Consumer trends

Market/Supply chain

Producers → Traders → Processors → Exporters/Importers → Retailers → Consumers
- International
- National
- Local

68 | *Producer Organisations: A Guide to Developing Collective Rural Enterprises*

In this context POs can play a critical role in mobilising small-scale producers to defend and promote their rights and in influencing the market environment on behalf of small-scale producers. Such action is usually called advocacy or lobbying. Case Study 8 provides a good example of POs' role in influencing the market environment.

Case Study 8: Asprepatía, Colombia

The production of panela, a brown sugar loaf made from sugar-cane that is used as a low-cost sweetener, is the main source of income for the rural population in the Patía region in western Colombia. A small amount of panela is produced industrially, but most production is based in small family-run units. In 2002, a group of private sugar mills applied for a licence to construct a very large panela mill in the Patía region. Although the proposed mill may have opened up new markets for panela produced in the region, its size was a threat to small-scale producers who risked being pushed out of the market. In response, a peasant farmer organisation, CIMA, mobilised small-scale producers to protest against the plan and defend their livelihoods. With the help of CIMA, an informal association of panela producers was formed to conduct the campaign and later in the year, the Ministry of Environment accepted the demands of the panela producers and rejected the plan to construct the mill.

The campaign against the panela mill prompted the producers involved in the informal association to address their weak position in the market chain. Their idea was to establish their own trading organisation that would trade directly with the panela wholesale markets. Asprepatía, the Association of Panela Producers of the Patía Region (Asociación de Paneleros de la Región del Patía), was formally registered as a non-profit association in 2004 and began trading with funds from a loan and member contributions. The aim of the organisation was to control the market price for panela by buying a large share of panela produced in the region. At the beginning, the association had difficulties buying enough panela because wholesalers often delayed their payments and many small-scale producers were not aware of the higher prices offered by the association. But with additional trading funds provided by Oxfam GB, Asprepatía was gradually able to increase its share of the market and has raised the market price paid to producers by over 30 per cent, while offering very competitive prices to wholesalers. At present the scale of the operation and the association's small profit margin is not big enough to cover its operational costs, which are funded by an Oxfam GB grant. It is anticipated that continued growth in the business will enable Asprepatía to cover its costs in three years' time, and offer much higher prices to producers on a competitive and sustainable basis.

Asprepatía has also successfully campaigned for the sector to adopt a standardised measurement unit for panela to ensure producers are paid fairly according to the actual weight. In the future it plans to increase the prices paid to small-scale producers further through organic certification and marketing panela to niche organic markets in the urban centres.

Asprepatía provides an example of a PO that was formed in response to a crisis in the market environment, which acted as a catalyst for a new initiative to improve panela producers' position in the market. Asprepatía has now gone on to improve the market environment for panela producers by campaigning for new standards that ensure producers are paid a fair price.

While problems in the market environment can provide the impulse for collective marketing activities through a PO, PO marketing activities can equally create the awareness, confidence, and incentives for producers to influence the market environment. In the case of NASFAM, the third-level, national organisation was created by second-level associations in order to increase the influence of small-scale producers on the national market environment. NASFAM has engaged in national policy debates on rural and economic development and successfully lobbied the government to exempt small-scale producers from the tobacco export tax, which means small-scale producers now receive a greater share of the export price. Similarly, the Palestinian olive-oil co-operatives are planning to create a second-level co-operative union that can promote and defend the interests of small-scale olive-oil producers in the Palestinian Olive Oil Council, which has always been dominated by large-scale producers.

AProCA, the Association of Cotton Producers of Africa (Association Des Producteurs De Coton Africains), is a regional association of national-level cotton-farmer associations across West and Central Africa. AProCA was established in 2004 by a group of national cotton-farmer leaders from six different countries in order to develop a common advocacy strategy on US cotton subsidies. With significant support from various NGOs, AProCA sent ten representatives to lobby for an end to Northern cotton subsidies at the 2005 World Trade Organisation Ministerial meeting, which agreed an end to cotton export subsidies in 2006. Although AProCA faces many challenges in developing a sustainable regional association that can effectively represent and promote the interests of cotton farmers in Africa, it provides a good example of the advocacy role POs can play at an international level.

Case Study 4 of UCASN provides an important example of the role played by NGOs and other organisations supporting POs in influencing the market environment in favour of small-scale producers. Association law in Mozambique requires new associations to go through a very bureaucratic and lengthy registration process and pay high registration fees. This has made it difficult for many informal POs to register as formal associations, which is necessary if they want to open bank accounts, access credit, and enter formal agreements in the market. In response, CLUSA and a number of NGOs and national associations have lobbied the government over a number of years, resulting in the introduction of a new law that involves a much simpler registration process and affordable registration fees.

These examples highlight the important role POs and supporting organisations can play in influencing the market environment. While POs can never afford to ignore the market environment, few POs have the capacity and resources to undertake advocacy work without external support. In all the above examples, the POs have relied on significant financial support as well as policy advice and training from donors, NGOs, and other agencies in order to carry out the advocacy work. Although AProCA aims to finance its activities in the long run through membership contributions, it still relies heavily on external grants.

Summary: influencing the market environment

- In the long term, POs can only develop into sustainable organisations that deliver real benefits to their members if they operate in a supportive market environment that protects their rights, reflects their interests, and enables them to compete in a fair environment.
- POs can play a very important role using their organisation, size, and networks to influence decision-makers at local, national, and international level.
- Effective lobbying and advocacy work requires significant skills and resources and few POs can develop and fund such activities without external support.

11 | Producer organisation development stages

As the above case studies have shown, POs are dynamic organisations that evolve over time, and in that process often change their structure, activities, and strategy. In this final chapter of Part II, we will consider whether all POs share a common development path and therefore whether they should all be aiming towards an ideal form or a common goal, in terms of their structure, business activities, and strategy. We will suggest that this is not a helpful way to approach a PO's development and instead identify a small set of universal capacities and characteristics which all POs need to pursue to become strong and sustainable POs, as defined in this guide.

A development model

Figure 11.1 presents a PO development path, starting with an informal, first-level organisation at an 'early stage' of development and ending with a three-level, national organisation, at an 'advanced stage' of development. This development path also involves a progression, from simple marketing activities of low-value commodities in local markets, to demanding processing and branding activities involving high-value products aimed at export markets.

While some POs do follow this path of development, it does not reflect the experience of many others, who see no reason to develop three levels of organisation and do not aim to enter export markets. Indeed, there are good reasons why many POs do not follow this path. For example:

- Many POs do not begin marketing low-value commodities and then diversify into high-value products. POs usually start by marketing whatever cash crop is produced by their members. In fact, the higher margins on high-value products can sometimes help POs establish their business at an early stage.

- The ideal size of a PO and its structure will depend on the needs of the business and the markets the PO is accessing. Big POs with complex structures are not necessarily more advanced than a small, single-level organisation. Agrolempa, for example, has remained a first-level association but achieves volume through the trading activities of the association-owned company.
- It is not possible or advantageous for all POs to get involved in processing and product branding as this depends on the nature of the product and the market the PO is targeting.
- Not all POs can undertake advocacy work as this will depend on the resources and capacity of the PO, the nature of the market environment, and whether other organisations are engaged in such activities.

An important principle for POs' development that emerges from these examples is the need for POs to find the right 'fit'. POs need to develop and adapt their structure, size, services, and strategy to find the best fit with their priorities and capacity, target market, and market environment. As the environment, markets, and priorities and capacity of POs change and evolve over time, POs need to constantly adapt to maintain a good fit between these factors. For example, Zadrima in Albania started off as an informal group of wine producers, who decided to help each other produce wine. Later, the group decided to establish a formal association in order to access the investment they needed to improve their processing

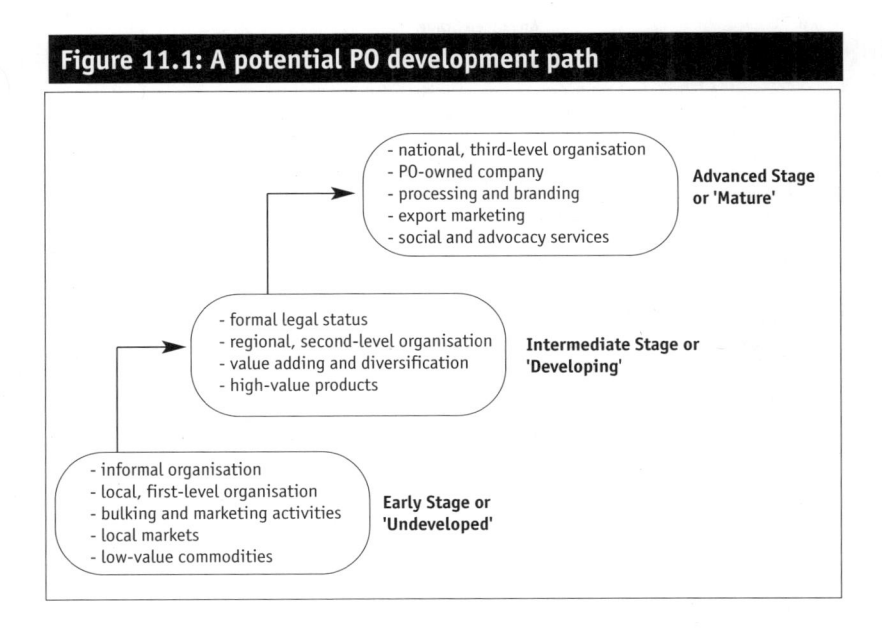

Figure 11.1: A potential PO development path

Advanced Stage or 'Mature':
- national, third-level organisation
- PO-owned company
- processing and branding
- export marketing
- social and advocacy services

Intermediate Stage or 'Developing':
- formal legal status
- regional, second-level organisation
- value adding and diversification
- high-value products

Early Stage or 'Undeveloped':
- informal organisation
- local, first-level organisation
- bulking and marketing activities
- local markets
- low-value commodities

Producer organisation development stages | 73

equipment. Then, once the business had become established, the members decided to register the PO as a co-operative to improve the credibility of the PO as a business. One potential characteristic of an 'advanced' PO therefore could be the ability to adapt its structure and business in response to the changing needs of its members and the demands of the market. Figure 11.2 identifies various capacities and practices in the governance and management of a PO at three progressive stages of development.

Although there are many aspects of a PO's business and its development that depend on the product, market, and local context, there are some more general indicators that mark the capacity and sustainability of a PO at different stages of development. Figure 11.3 lists some of these indicators for a PO's business and service development at three broad stages of development.

Figure 11.2: Producer organisation governance and management at different stages of development

(A) Strong grassroots trust and confidence in leadership
(B) Routine change of elected leaders
(C) Women and other minority groups participate in leadership
(D) Strong ownership and sense of responsibility for the PO
(E) Leaders have capacity and experience to control the business
(F) PO is very responsive and can manage change effectively

Advanced Stage

(A) General trust in the work of leaders and managers
(B) Occasional to frequent change in elected leaders
(C) Women and minority groups participate in decision-making
(D) Growing sense of ownership over many of the PO's activities
(E) Leaders have some ability to monitor and control the business
(F) PO able to respond to some changes in the PO and in the market

Intermediate Stage

(A) Weak trust and confidence in leadership and management
(B) No rotation or change in elected leaders
(C) Women and minority groups excluded from active decision-making
(D) Weak sense of ownership over PO's activities
(E) Leaders have weak control over the business and its managers
(F) PO is unable to adapt to changes in the PO and in the market

Early Stage

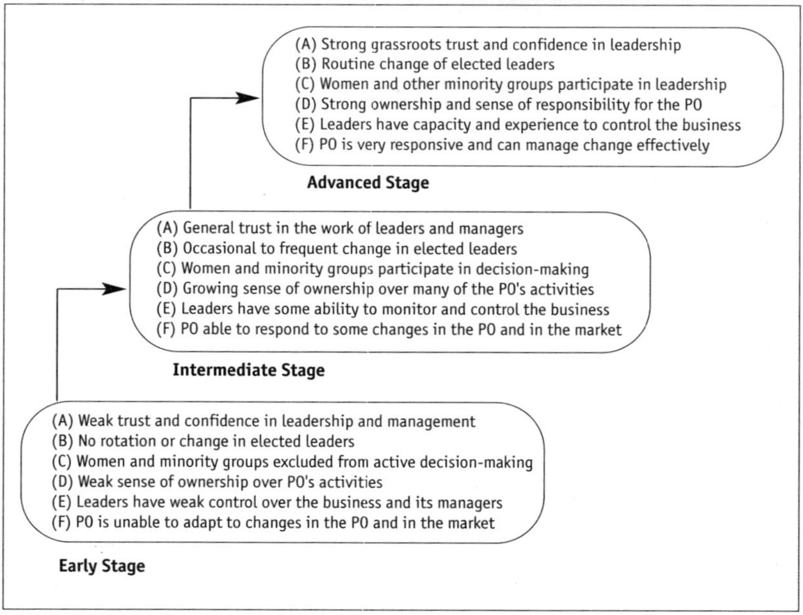

Figure 11.3: Producer organisation business development at different stages of development

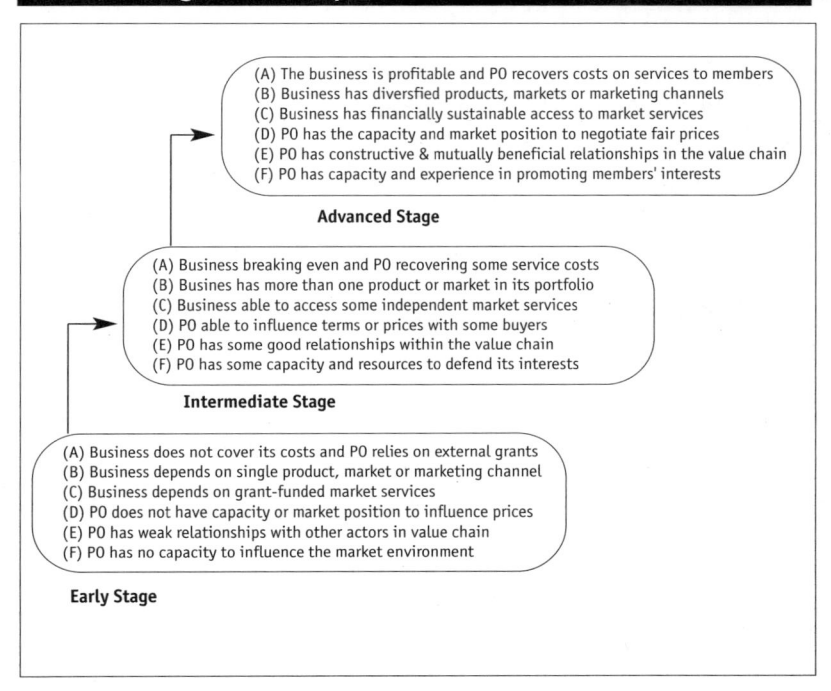

(A) The business is profitable and PO recovers costs on services to members
(B) Business has diversfied products, markets or marketing channels
(C) Business has financially sustainable access to market services
(D) PO has the capacity and market position to negotiate fair prices
(E) PO has constructive & mutually beneficial relationships in the value chain
(F) PO has capacity and experience in promoting members' interests

Advanced Stage

(A) Business breaking even and PO recovering some service costs
(B) Busines has more than one product or market in its portfolio
(C) Business able to access some independent market services
(D) PO able to influence terms or prices with some buyers
(E) PO has some good relationships within the value chain
(F) PO has some capacity and resources to defend its interests

Intermediate Stage

(A) Business does not cover its costs and PO relies on external grants
(B) Business depends on single product, market or marketing channel
(C) Business depends on grant-funded market services
(D) PO does not have capacity or market position to influence prices
(E) PO has weak relationships with other actors in value chain
(F) PO has no capacity to influence the market environment

Early Stage

Most POs will probably have a mixture of capacities and practices in different areas: some that are weak and are associated with the early stage of development, others that are at the intermediate stage, and even some associated with the advanced stage. Given the scale of the challenges facing small-scale producers it may often take many years before a PO develops all the capacities and practices associated with an 'advanced' or 'mature' PO. The important challenge for POs and those working with POs is to ensure that the organisation is moving in the right direction and is making steady, if slow, progress in all these areas. Few POs will have the capacity and energy to focus on each dimension of development at the same time, and those working with POs must therefore learn to support and live with the tension of organisations that have a very mixed set of capacities and practices. One important implication of these development stages is that it generally takes many years and considerable investments before POs are able to play a significant role in the market and fill some of the gaps left by market liberalisation. NGO and donor policies and investments therefore need to recognise the considerable length of time required before POs can help overcome at least some of the many market failures that small-scale producers face in today's liberalised and globalised markets.

> **Summary: development stages**
>
> - There is no universal development path for POs and the key challenge for POs is to find the right 'fit' between their structure, activities, and strategy, on the one hand, and the changing needs and capacity of their members and the changing demands of the market, on the other.
> - There are a set of basic capacities and practices that all POs need to work on and develop if they want to become strong and sustainable organisations and businesses.

Part I of the guide provided a background to POs and the rationale for POs. Part II provided an overview of POs, what they look like, and how they operate, and in this final chapter we have begun to consider PO development issues: how POs need to develop to become strong organisations and businesses. In Part III, we turn to the role of development NGOs and how they can enable POs to develop into strong businesses and organisations which empower small-scale producers in the market.

Part III | Working with Producer Organisations

Orienting questions

What role should development NGOs play in supporting the development of POs?

What basic principles should guide development NGOs' work with POs?

What issues do development NGOs need to consider before they start working with POs?

What essential capacity do POs need to develop to enable them to become strong businesses and organisations, and how can development NGOs support this development process?

How can development NGOs help POs implement more difficult and challenging activities?

What are the main issues and challenges development NGOs need to consider when forming new POs?

The aim of Part III is to provide a general overview of the main steps, methods, and challenges involved in facilitating the development of POs, and to identify when development NGOs need to draw on specialist expertise and support. This part aims to be practical but it does not provide step-by-step, technical guidance as it is directed at staff of development NGOs whose main role will be facilitating, funding, or co-ordinating the support process rather than directly implementing support activities. For more detailed technical guidance on issues such as marketing, accounting, or business development, the reader will need to consult specialist agencies or one of the many existing manuals and guidebooks on these topics. The guidance and insights in Part III draw on lessons from the case studies presented in Part II of the guide, as well as on a wide range of other materials and contributions.[39]

Below, we will first consider the role and approach of development NGOs, before looking at basic issues that need to be addressed before beginning to work with POs. The following three chapters take a closer look at the process of developing PO capacity, paying particular attention to the issues and challenges development NGOs need to consider at each stage of the process.

12 | The role of development NGOs

In this chapter we will identify what strategic roles development NGOs can play in the support process. To identify these roles we first need to consider the role of other actors and the main strengths and weaknesses of development NGOs in supporting POs.

Organisations supporting producer organisations

There are many actors that do business with POs, such as traders, input suppliers, and banks, but their main aim is not to support the development of POs as businesses or organisations. In the introduction to this guide we identified four different actors, apart from development NGOs, that provide direct support to help POs develop. The following is a brief description of these four actors and their potential strengths and weaknesses in supporting POs:

1. *Specialist support agencies:* these are commercial or not-for-profit agencies, such as CLUSA (Co-operative League of the USA) or SNV (Netherlands Development Organisation), or individual consultants who specialise in developing POs and providing technical support on business or organisational development. These agencies usually have considerable expertise and experience in supporting POs and their integration into market or value chains. Because of their strong focus on developing sustainable businesses, such agencies may focus their support only on small-scale producers who have the potential to produce high-value products that meet market demands.

2. *Government agencies:* in many countries, government agencies such as the ministries of agriculture, or co-operative promotion offices provide support to POs, either through specific support programmes, targeted at POs, or by providing an 'enabling environment' for POs to develop.

The support provided by government agencies is critical for POs because their authority, reach, and resources can enable them to address fundamental problems in the market and market environment. However, government agencies are rarely able to respond to the particular needs and priorities of individual POs and are often driven by the interests of more influential business groups.

3. *Private companies and Alternative Trading Organisations (ATOs):* exporters, processing companies, and ATOs, such as Twin Trading (UK) or GEPA (Germany), sometimes provide specific support to POs in their supply chains to ensure they have the capacity to supply the required quantity and quality of products. ATOs, in particular, often invest in this type of support and some even have special PO support units. As companies, these actors have a first-hand understanding of market demands and business-development priorities and ATOs usually also have expertise in developing the capacity of POs. However ATOs and, in particular, exporters tend to limit their support to POs that are already participating in an export supply chain or have the potential to supply new products demanded by export markets.

4. *Donors:* many international donors, such as the International Fund for Agricultural Development (IFAD) or the United States Agency for International Development (USAID), provide support either directly to POs or, more commonly, to specialist support agencies working with POs, sometimes via government agencies. CLUSA's PO support programme in Mozambique, for example, is funded by USAID. Donors often have considerable resources for PO support activities although, like development NGOs, their funding priorities can change quickly.

Strengths and weaknesses of development NGOs in supporting producer organisations

In contrast to specialist support agencies and ATOs, development NGOs, like Oxfam GB, usually lack business and market expertise and experience. Many, if not most, staff tend to have a social development background and therefore lack the expertise to support a PO's business effectively. Some staff may prefer to see POs as a means of channelling resources to resource-poor producers rather than as commercial structures and some may even have reservations about promoting POs.

Oxfam GB's experience in Mozambique highlights this problem. In Mozambique, Oxfam GB has been supporting the PO UCASN (see Case Study 4, in Part II) for many years. One of the challenges for Oxfam GB and UCASN has been the lack of continuity in Oxfam's support programme. When Oxfam first started working with UCASN, its country staff were committed to supporting POs as a means of promoting rural development, although few staff had business development experience. For this reason, Oxfam GB negotiated support from a specialist support agency to help develop UCASN's marketing capacity. However, after some years the relationship with UCASN and the specialist support agency deteriorated as new Oxfam GB staff did not share the same commitment to supporting POs and instead favoured alternative development strategies. Since then these problems have been addressed, but this example highlights some of the difficulties development NGOs can face in supporting POs.

Despite these significant gaps, development NGOs often have considerable experience and expertise to offer the PO support process. Development NGOs tend to have a good understanding of local social and economic development issues and the needs and priorities of local communities and small-scale producers. Many NGOs have a long-term commitment to, and good relationships with, local communities based on trust. They often support a wide range of development projects that address development problems from different angles, including, for example, work on local governance or on gender relations. Development NGOs are also often well-placed to address wider development and market problems and to work to develop an enabling environment for POs that ensures a greater number of producers can be supported through limited resources. These factors can enable development NGOs to play an important mediating and facilitating role in the PO support process.

For example, in India, Oxfam GB has been supporting an emerging network of POs involved in marketing non-timber forest products. Oxfam GB, alongside various organisations, has been supporting the new structure. One of the problems was that commercial market service providers who were hired to support the development of the business did not understand the local context and needs of the producers. Oxfam GB staff therefore had to play an important role mediating between these service providers and the PO, helping the service providers to adapt their market services to the particular context and challenges of the PO and its members. Drawing on its capacity development experience and contacts in other development programmes, Oxfam GB also helped to develop the contacts and confidence of the new PO by supporting exchanges with POs in other regions and sectors.

Different support approaches

Hands-on approach versus support facilitation

Development NGOs can take many different approaches to supporting POs. In the above example from India, Oxfam GB's approach was to facilitate support provided by other specialist agencies. However, development NGOs can also take a more hands-on approach, developing the capacity of POs directly and even taking over the management of some of their activities. This approach can be attractive because it gives the NGO more control over the support process and its investment and may also deliver faster results. The case study of OAPI in India (see Case Study 7, Chapter 8) provides an example of a very hands-on approach to developing POs. In this example, Oxfam GB has taken a major shareholding in a farmer trading company that will manage the processing and onward sale of seed cotton supplied by a group of farmer co-operatives. There were two main reasons for this approach. Firstly, the farmer co-operatives are still growing and do not have the capacity to manage a trading company, but the co-operatives need a trading company in order to access higher prices and reverse the growing destitution and indebtedness among their members. Secondly, Oxfam GB's equity investment can help the new company access additional financing from the market. However, while in certain circumstances there may be special reasons for taking a more hands-on approach, in most cases, there are good reasons why development NGOs should focus on a facilitating role, linking POs to other service providers, based on the following arguments:

- Development NGOs may have specialist staff, but the majority tend to lack experience and expertise in many critical areas of PO development and therefore do not have the capacity to support PO development directly on their own.

- According to our definition in Part I, we are aiming to promote producer-owned and controlled organisations, i.e. organisations that are driven by the priorities and objectives of their members and that develop organically based on their members' decisions, actions, and experience. A hands-on approach can reduce the initial risk faced by producers, as in the case of OAPI, but it also risks weakening members' ownership over the PO.

- Providing support directly to POs and getting closely involved in managing the development process can undermine POs' sustainability and risk increasing their dependence on a development NGO. For example, an NGO in Mozambique has provided support and market services to POs directly, including grants for running costs and input services, rather than trying to link POs to potential financial- and input-service providers in the area. While this support has enabled the PO to make rapid progress in its marketing activities, it has increased its dependency on the development NGO, as its business relies on the NGO's market services.

One way of understanding this facilitating role is to see it as a partnership between the development NGO and the PO. A partnership is based on a shared mission and the belief that both parties have equal importance in the relationship, although this does not mean that both have the same power: NGOs' role as donor, for example, can give them considerable influence over POs. The challenge for development NGOs is not to use this power in a way that undermines the independence and development of the PO. Instead of controlling the PO and its development, the aim should be to develop a relationship based on mutual trust that enables both the NGO and the PO to be frank about their interests and resolve differences.

Balancing social versus business objectives

Throughout this guide we have emphasised that POs are rural businesses. In order to survive they must pursue financial sustainability as a primary objective. This can be difficult to accept for development NGOs, whose overall mission is to eradicate poverty through inclusive community-based development. NGO staff are likely to be eager to use their resources to find immediate solutions to producers' marketing problems, for example, by providing grants for processing equipment or running costs without considering how the PO will cover these costs in the long term. NGOs may also want to encourage POs to use their profits to support separate social activities or to provide their services on a more inclusive basis, for example, extending the PO's services to all members of the community. In Southern Africa, for example, an NGO encouraged a PO to offer the input services provided by its second-level organisation to all members in the local community. However, as PO members in the first-level organisation only received small benefits from participating in the PO, there was little reason for them to remain members as they could access the most important services provided by the PO without being a member. As a result the sustainability of the whole PO was threatened. These examples highlight how NGOs' good intentions can weaken or even undermine POs' businesses, threatening their survival and therefore potential to generate business or social benefits for anyone. As POs develop they may generate surplus resources that can enable them to respond to social needs beyond those of their members, but such activities should not be encouraged too soon, and are best managed separately from the PO's business. The example of COMUCAP, discussed in Chapter 5, illustrates the difficulty of combining social and business activities within the same structure. Ultimately, prioritising financial sustainability means that development NGOs have to allow POs with little prospect of becoming viable businesses to fail.

Scope of support

Many NGOs focus their support on individual POs and help the PO access markets and existing service providers. If the market system (i.e. the system involving the market or value chain, market services, and the market environment) that the PO is accessing is working well and there are no problems in the market environment, this approach may be adequate. However, as we have noted earlier in the guide, POs often face fundamental market problems. These include buyer-driven value chains, exploitative traders, unfair competition through partially liberalised trade policies, unfavourable legal frameworks, and a lack of essential government services. Development NGOs will need to explore ways of addressing these wider problems, through complementary activities, if they really want to help PO members benefit from market access.

The strategic role of development NGOs

Based on the considerations above, we identify the following five strategic roles for development NGOs in the PO support process:

1. *Accompaniment:* although there are sometimes many actors offering support to POs, few have the resources or a commitment to support POs and their development over many years. Development NGOs can therefore often play a crucial role as a PO's long-term development partner, supporting and 'accompanying' the development of the organisation and business. Development NGOs will be able to provide some capacity development assistance where their staff have expertise, for example in developing the capacity of grassroots members and strengthening the PO's governance structure. However, their main role is to help POs analyse and identify their development needs and priorities and together develop a support strategy. For example, in Viet Nam, Oxfam GB has acted as the Clam Clubs' main partner organisation, supporting their growth at each stage of development.

2. *Mobilising and co-ordinating support activities:* development NGOs may either work with a PO as their only development partner, or alongside other actors. In either case, development NGOs can play a critical role mobilising and co-ordinating the necessary support from specialist support agencies, government agencies, and other actors.

Development NGOs can also use their status and contacts to leverage financial support from donors, financial institutions, or other sources. For example, in Mozambique, Oxfam GB has mobilised and co-ordinated support for the PO UCASN from donors and specialist support agencies.

3. *Facilitating chain co-ordination:* although development NGOs do not have the experience or authority to co-ordinate the activities of different players in a market or value chain, they can act as a catalyst to bring together different players in the chain, build trust, and facilitate dialogue and negotiation between POs, suppliers, and buyers, as a basis for improved co-ordination. For example, in St Lucia, Oxfam GB organised a conference that brought together POs, hotels, the government, and other players in order to find ways of overcoming past failed attempts of hotels to purchase fresh produce from local farmers rather than from the USA.

4. *Lobbying for change:* POs often face fundamental problems in the market and market environment that require changes in national and international market structures and economic and development policies. Development NGOs can play a crucial role advocating with and on behalf of POs to bring about these critical changes. For example, Oxfam GB supported the new regional association of cotton POs in West and Central Africa, AProCA, in its efforts to challenge US cotton subsidies at the World Trade Organisation, and Oxfam GB is working with other organisations to lobby for a change in the laws governing POs in Viet Nam.

5. *Promoting a development perspective:* at the same time as recognising the need to prioritise POs' business objectives, development NGOs can play an important role in raising social-development issues in their work with POs and other service providers. As development NGOs usually support POs within a wider development programme, they can draw on experience in other development projects and implement complementary development activities to support ongoing work with POs. For example, in the Dominican Republic Oxfam GB has provided support to women members of Fedecares, a federation of coffee producers, by organising meetings for women and supporting leadership training.

Development NGOs will often support POs in other ways, depending on the expertise of individual staff and the challenges of the particular context. However, we suggest that development NGOs can, in general, make a strategic and, perhaps, the most valuable contribution to supporting POs by focusing their efforts and resources on the five strategic roles described above. To reflect the focus in all these roles on facilitation we will use the term 'facilitating agency' (FA) from now on to refer to development NGOs or other agencies that play this facilitating role in the support process.

To conclude this chapter, the following box identifies a set of basic support principles that should guide FAs' work with POs.

Summary: PO support principles

- *Develop independent capacity:* support activities should focus on developing the capacity of POs to manage and implement their activities independently. Facilitating agencies should therefore avoid implementing or managing any activities *for* POs unless: (i) there are strong reasons for doing so that are supported by and are in the long-term interests of producers (see for example Case Study 7, Chapter 8); (ii) the FA, at the same time, builds the capacity of the PO to take over those activities; and (iii) both the FA and the PO have agreed a clear process and timetable for handing over management and implementation to the PO.

- *Promote independence:* the support provided by the FA and its relationship with the PO should respect and encourage the PO's organisational independence, and FAs should therefore promote internal accountability between PO leaders and grassroots members before external accountability to the FA.

- *Prioritise the business:* FAs should prioritise developing a sustainable business above social objectives that may undermine the PO's financial sustainability.

- *Promote long-term sustainability:* all support activities should contribute to the financial and/or organisational sustainability of the PO, directly or indirectly. From the very start FAs should therefore approach all their support work with a clear exit strategy in mind and a joint plan agreed with the PO that sets out how the PO will become financially sustainable.

- *Adopt a co-ordinated approach:* few FAs have the necessary resources and expertise to support POs effectively on their own and even if they do, a PO's independence can suffer if it only relates to a single supporting organisation. A co-ordinated approach, involving a wide range of actors, therefore lies at the heart of an effective PO support strategy.

- *Take a long-term approach:* FAs need to recognise and accept that supporting independent POs along these lines is a long-term activity, which requires patience and a willingness to accept that

POs' development paths will not always be optimal from the point of view of the FA. For example, women gaining decision-making and leadership roles may require a change in attitude and beliefs, which takes time.

- *Set realistic expectations:* FAs need to be realistic about the expected results of their support activities, particularly in regions with limited competitive advantages. FAs also need to ensure that POs have realistic expectations about the level and type of support the FA will offer.

- *Understand the market system:* FAs' support needs to be based on a sound understanding of the market system. In this way FAs can help POs invest their limited resources in viable business and marketing strategies.

- *Allow failure:* as POs' long-term success depends on the viability of their business, FAs have to resist the temptation to support POs that would otherwise have no chance of succeeding as a business in the long term.

13 | Initial steps and considerations

Before beginning any work with POs, facilitating agencies (FAs) need to conduct a careful assessment of producers, existing POs, markets, the market environment and their own capacity in order to decide how best to support POs. In particular, FAs will need to make the following important decisions:

1. If some of the minimum conditions for PO development are not present, whether to focus first on alternative activities to create the necessary conditions for successful PO development, rather than supporting POs directly, e.g. lobbying for a supportive legal framework.

2. Whether to invest in complementary development activities, alongside supporting POs, to assist their development and promote wider access to the benefits of POs, e.g. developing the production assets and skills of small-scale producers so they can produce a reliable surplus.

3. Whether to postpone PO support activities, for example if they are not likely to be economically viable or benefit small-scale producers, directly or indirectly, for the foreseeable future (e.g. in very poor rural areas with chronic food insecurity).

The different assessments described in this chapter are also important because they enable FAs to judge what resources and time-commitment are necessary to help POs develop into strong, producer-owned organisations and financially sustainable businesses. For example, in a region where markets are thin and there is a low level of entrepreneurial initiative or managerial capacity among producers due to a history of relief interventions, developing strong POs is likely to take much longer and require far greater investments than in an area with relatively well-developed markets and in which producers are already market-oriented.

Assessing minimum conditions

To develop into sustainable businesses and organisations POs require certain minimum conditions in the market environment and within their organisation. When these are not present, POs may need more support and much more time to develop into strong, independent organisations. This has implications for the role and resources of FAs. Some of the main minimum conditions that FAs need to consider are identified below.

Market environment

- *Security:* like any other business, POs need a minimum level of security in order to operate effectively. Even low levels of conflict or unrest can significantly increase the costs and risks of doing business and reduce the profitability and competitiveness of the PO's business. The olive-oil co-operatives in Palestine, for example, have to cope with considerable insecurity, including violent unrest and frequent border closures that block access to international markets. To enable the co-operatives to develop under these conditions, Oxfam GB and other organisations have had to take on many of the business risks by providing grants for investments and brokering marketing channels for the co-operatives.
- *Economic stability:* although economic instability affects all businesses, the impact is likely to be greatest on small-scale producers operating in poor rural markets or involved in export markets, especially during their early stages of development. For example, high interest rates in Malawi make it very difficult for businesses like NASFAM to compete against foreign companies with access to cheap loans outside the country.
- *Political independence:* as demonstrated by the failure of many state-led co-operative-promotion programmes in the past, to succeed, POs need to be able to operate without political interference in their management. In Indonesia, many co-operatives were used by the ruling party as a means of delivering rural services and are a long way from being producer-owned businesses.
- *Suitable legal framework:* POs need a supporting legal framework that allows them to register easily and choose a legal structure that suits their circumstances and offers some competitive advantages, such as lower tax rates. For example, the development of the Clam Clubs in Viet Nam is constrained by the lack of appropriate legal structures for the POs.
- *Minimal level of market development:* when markets are very thin and the cost of doing business and accessing markets is very high then it may be very difficult, if not impossible, for POs to become financially sustainable without large-scale investments by the state in infrastructure and rural development. Food markets across sub-Saharan Africa, for example,

are often very weak because of poor infrastructure and dependence on rain-fed production and POs alone will not overcome these fundamental constraints.

- *Competitive market structure:* producers are unlikely to benefit significantly from POs if the markets they access are not competitive and are fundamentally biased against small-scale producers. For example, while NASFAM has enabled small-scale tobacco producers in Malawi to cut out local traders and access auction prices directly, these prices are heavily influenced by a handful of multinational companies who control the global market.

Producers

- *Production capacity:* many small-scale producers face fundamental constraints that limit their ability to produce a reliable surplus, including lack of land, labour, or irrigation. Unless these constraints are addressed through a wide range of investments by the state and other actors, POs offer few benefits to these producers.
- *Independent initiative:* in Chapter 7 we looked at various factors that affect the governance of POs including independent initiative. Whether FAs are planning to support existing POs or facilitate the development of new organisations, their long-term development is likely to depend critically on the extent to which they are based on producers' initiatives.
- *Social capital:* POs' sustainability also depends on the level of trust and understanding between members and elected leaders. POs with limited social capital within the group will find it harder to cope with difficult times and agree common objectives. FAs will need considerable skills, patience, and resources to help the members develop this trust and understanding over time.
- *Membership capacity:* developing the capacity of PO members should be an important priority for FAs but the support process will be much more challenging if few or none of the producers have basic business or management experience. For example, Oxfam GB in Albania has had to invest considerable time and resources to help the members of Zadrima to develop their wine business, as most of the members had little previous business experience.

Rapid market and producer assessment

FAs need to have a good understanding of local markets and producers in order to provide effective support to POs in a particular region. FAs need to know about:

- the livelihoods, production, and marketing strategies of small-scale producers (both men and women) in the region;
- Supply and demand at the local, national, or international level compared to the potential production and marketing capacity of small-scale producers in the region;
- sub-sectors (e.g. fresh fruit or honey) that have the greatest potential for small-scale producers as well as sub-sectors where small-scale producers may have a competitive advantage;
- the constraints small-scale producers face in competing in and benefiting from local market or value chains;
- existing POs in the region, their capacity and effectiveness;
- government agencies, private companies, specialist support agencies, NGOs, or other actors operating in the region and the market services and assistance they offer small-scale producers and POs as well as the challenges they may pose.

As we will see in Chapter 14, all POs need to conduct an assessment of local markets, their competitors, and service providers in order to develop a business strategy. FAs' rapid market assessment, described in this section, is not meant to replace POs' own market research. Instead, the aim is for the FA to develop a general understanding of local market opportunities and constraints and the capacity of producers and service providers so that the FA can identify the main problems facing small-scale producers in the region and how best to support POs in the short, medium, and long term.

In many cases, FAs will need to hire specialists to conduct the market assessment, but FA staff may need guidance in order to manage this process and ensure important development concerns are taken into account (e.g. the capacity and needs of poorer small-scale producers or a gender perspective). Annex 2 provides a checklist of the important questions and issues that a rapid market and producer assessment should address. The further reading and resources section in Annex 1 lists some useful resources on market assessment tools and methodologies.

Work with existing producer organisations or form a new one?

Once an FA has decided to promote POs, it may need to decide whether to work with existing POs, however informal the groups are, or to set up a new PO from scratch. The first step should always be to investigate what POs, if any, there are in the area and to develop some idea about their objectives, activities, and capacity. The checklist in Annex 2 lists the main questions that an assessment of existing POs needs to address. If there are no POs or none that need the FA's support, the FA may consider setting up a new PO. However, establishing a new PO is a challenging task and should not be undertaken lightly as the following case study from Georgia illustrates.

Case Study 9: Kiwi Growers' Co-operative, Georgia

In 2002, a micro-finance organisation funded by Oxfam GB in Georgia began a pilot micro-credit project. The project provided group loans to smallholder farmers with the aim of increasing agricultural production and promoting market access. The micro-finance organisation organised two groups of farmers producing kiwis for the local market and provided group loans and additional financial support. The organisation's project staff co-ordinated the collection of the kiwis from the group members' farms and the transport to markets in the capital. The aim was to help farmers access better prices by selling the kiwis directly to wholesalers and in the main markets of Tbilisi.

These initial marketing activities proved successful and the farmers were eager to develop the initiative. This led to the creation of a PO, a joint liability company (a type of private company in which shareholders are personally liable for the company's debts), with 22 farmers as shareholders and an elected board of directors. However, the organisation's staff effectively managed all aspects of the business and the members merely followed the instructions of project staff. With time, the farmers began to get more involved in decision-making and initiated new marketing activities; however, tensions began to emerge within the PO. A growing number of members preferred to receive individual loans for production, rather than the joint loan provided to the PO. Some members were also unhappy about the legal status of the PO as there was a big difference in the contributions of individual members and they risked losing their personal assets if the PO failed. Some of the more entrepreneurial and productive members believed they would gain more and risk less by working on their own. As the collective marketing strategy was no longer supported by many of the members, the PO could no longer operate effectively and the collective initiative collapsed.

In order to become sustainable organisations and businesses, POs have to have a strong foundation of producer ownership and initiative. As the experience in Georgia demonstrates, this initiative and sense of ownership may be weak or absent when POs are set up by external organisations. In fact, the more an FA is identified with the formation of the PO, the less likely it is that members will feel responsible for the success of the organisation. In the case of the kiwi growers in Georgia, the NGO invested considerable resources in developing the PO but from the start the NGO's staff were the driving force behind the initiative. Initially, when things went well the members were happy to support the organisation but when problems arose it was clear that the farmers had little interest in making the collective action work. The risks involved in forming POs are particularly high for development NGOs, especially if they have implemented relief or social-development activities in the same communities in the past. In this case, it can be difficult to judge whether producers really want to organise themselves as a result of their own initiative to address problems in the market, or whether they view the PO, primarily, as a means of accessing external assistance. Forming new POs is therefore a difficult process that requires considerable sensitivity, skills, and experience. Where possible, FAs should try to work with existing POs and help develop their capacity, rather than creating new organisations. Chapter 16 provides further guidance on forming new POs.

Assessing potential gender and poverty impact

We have stressed throughout this guide that POs cannot be treated as a straightforward development tool to strengthen the livelihoods of small-scale producers. In fact, as we suggested in Chapter 4, POs will often provide few, if any, direct or indirect benefits to a significant number of poorer producers, during their early years of development. For POs to become sustainable it is important that FAs recognise and accept these limitations and do not push POs to pursue separate social objectives. Nonetheless, it is important that FAs develop some idea, from the start, about which types or groups of producers are likely to benefit, directly and indirectly, from POs, and which producers are likely to be excluded and why. The aim of this exercise is to highlight the potential gaps in any PO support project, in terms of its impact on poverty and gender. At the very least, this should enable FAs to:

- be more realistic about what their support activities can achieve and build consensus within the FA to avoid disruptive changes in strategy at a later stage (e.g. Oxfam GB's experience in Mozambique described in the previous chapter);

- assess the constraints, including time, cash, skills, confidence, or social norms, which may prevent women from participating in and benefiting from POs. Based on this, FAs will need to consider what strategies and additional activities may be necessary to create the conditions for women to participate equally in PO activities, e.g. whether it may be necessary to promote women-only POs or work on gender relations within the household;

- identify what complementary development activities are likely to be required over the course of the support project to increase the direct and indirect benefits of POs, e.g. to develop the skills and production capacity of poorer semi-subsistence producers;

- co-ordinate their activities with other agencies, including government departments, NGOs, and specialist support agencies, to ensure these issues and more fundamental problems are addressed, e.g. to get the regional government to invest in small-scale irrigation projects that benefit poorer small-scale producers.

Information collected from the rapid market and producer assessment, and existing poverty or gender assessments conducted by the FA or other NGOs, should help FAs to consider these issues.

Exit strategies

To enable POs to become independent organisations and financially sustainable businesses, FAs need to plan all their support work with a clear exit strategy that is agreed and understood by both parties. In practice, FAs often begin supporting POs without thinking about when or how they will be able to withdraw their support, as Case Study 10 highlights.

Case Study 10: Aprainores, El Salvador

From 1996, Oxfam GB began working with Aprainores, the Agro-Industrial Association of Organic Producers of El Salvador (La Asociación de Productores Agroindustriales Orgánicos de El Salvador), based in San Vicente province of El Salvador. The main economic activity of the producers is cashew-nut production and Aprainores processes their organic cashew nuts for the export market.

For the first six years of its work with Aprainores, Oxfam GB provided support to the PO but also acted as a trading partner, importing and retailing the cashew nuts through its Fair Trade programme. In 2002, however, Oxfam GB decided to stop acting as an importer whilst retaining the retail function. This came as a shock to the members of Aprainores as they were unsure whether their business could develop alternative export trading partners.

To assist the transition process, Oxfam GB supported Aprainores in the development of a new business plan, including the development of new customers by participating in trade fairs, such as BioFach, a large organic trade fair held in Germany every year. Further investments enabled the PO to increase its membership in order to make better use of its existing processing plant, which until then had not been fully utilised. By 2005, Aprainores was a profitable business with multiple new and existing customers, but despite this progress the PO still faces challenges. As a result of its previous dependence on Oxfam GB and another specialist support agency, the members' sense of ownership over the PO is still weak and the PO still faces difficulties in managing the business independently.

The example of Aprainores highlights the difficulties FAs and other supporting organisations can face when they provide support to POs without a clear exit strategy. These difficulties can be even greater when the FA takes on core business activities that the PO depends on to conduct its business, such as acting as an exporter. For this reason it is essential that FAs develop a clear exit strategy from the very start with the POs they are supporting. An exit strategy should be based on the support principles outlined in the previous chapter and needs to consider the following questions:

- What fundamental changes in the market and market environment are necessary for the PO to become a viable business that benefits its members? How realistic is it to expect that the FA, along with other actors, can contribute to these changes in the foreseeable future?
- What capacity does the PO need to develop in order to become financially sustainable and to manage its business independently?
- How can the FA help the PO to develop this capacity without encouraging dependency on the FA's resources, advice, or support services?
- What does the FA need to do to ensure that, in the long term, the PO can access trade partners and market services independently of the FA?
- What investments and approaches are necessary and approximately how long will it take for the PO to become a financially sustainable business? Can the FA mobilise the necessary resources and sustain its support over this time period?
- How does the FA need to phase its support so it can gradually withdraw its support and allow the PO to operate independently?

Ideally, an exit strategy will involve a withdrawal in several stages in which the FA gradually reduces its involvement. This may also include a gradual change in focus in terms of the FA's support. Figure 13.1 provides an example of a three-stage support process and exit strategy for a large PO, with three levels of organisation. This is just one example and each FA needs to develop its own strategy in consultation with each PO it plans to support.

Figure 13.1: An example of an exit strategy with different phases of support[40]

Stage I (e.g. years 1-3)	Stage II (e.g. years 3-6)	Stage III (e.g. years 6-8)
The FA works with one or two POs in order to develop the capacity of their first-level organisations and increase the FA's understanding of the local context and the needs of POs.	FA steps back from close involvement with first-level POs and instead focuses on facilitating market linkages and access to service providers and supporting second-level POs.	FA focuses its work on developing the capacity of third-level POs and of specific business services and improving the efficiency of specific market chains.

Assessing support capacity

It should be clear by now that supporting POs effectively requires significant resources and commitment on the part of FAs. Even established and successful POs, such as NASFAM in Malawi or Agrolempa in El Salvador, still require significant support from FAs many years after they were first established. It is therefore important for FAs to assess carefully whether they have the necessary capacity and organisational commitment to support POs effectively. FAs should consider the following questions:

- Do FA staff have a good theoretical and practical understanding of rural markets and businesses and the challenges faced by small-scale producers?
- What marketing strategies are likely to be necessary for small-scale producers to benefit from market access and what implications may this have for the required timeframe and scale of support?
- Does the FA have established contacts with a wide range of local and regional service providers and specialists that have the necessary technical knowledge, practical experience, and training skills to develop the capacity of the PO?
- Does the FA have good relations with local and regional government departments that provide services to small-scale producers or POs?
- Does the FA have sufficient financial and human resources to help facilitate the support process until the PO has become a sustainable organisation and business?
- Does the FA have a long-term institutional commitment to supporting POs that will not be affected by changes to staff, organisational priorities, or donor funding?

Negotiating a support relationship

Agreeing a support strategy

At the beginning, when an FA first starts working with a PO, the support relationship is likely to be informal as both organisations are still getting to know each other. However, it is important that FAs communicate their aims clearly and that they clarify the terms of any support provided to the PO from the very start. Once a certain level of understanding and trust has developed, it is useful for both parties to formalise the support relationship based on a jointly agreed support strategy. This process should lead to a clear understanding by both parties concerning:

1. The basic principles and values on which the support relationship is based;
2. The main objectives of the partnership;
3. The role and approach of the FA;
4. The scale and type of support the PO can expect from the FA;
5. The support priorities for the coming period;
6. Any actions or commitments the FA expects from the PO;
7. The timeframe for the FA's support, including different stages of support and the FA's exit strategy.

This can be captured in a service agreement or contract, defining the terms and conditions of the support services, or a memorandum of understanding (MOU), clarifying the purpose of the support relationship and defining each party's rights and responsibilities. The resulting agreement should be reviewed and, if necessary, re-negotiated by both parties on a regular basis to reflect the changing nature of the partnership and the changing needs and priorities of both parties. This formal clarification of the partnership is important but it must be recognised that contracts or MOUs do not reduce the need for FAs to manage and invest in their relationship with POs on a continuous basis. Effective partnerships ultimately depend on honest communication and trust, which require time and effort.

Assessing capacity and support priorities

A support strategy needs to be based on a shared understanding of the PO's capacity-development needs, and the FA therefore needs to develop an accurate understanding, with the PO, of the PO's strengths and weaknesses at every level of the organisation and business. This understanding can only develop with time if and as the trust and openness between both parties grows. Annex 3 provides an overview of the different areas of capacity that need to be considered by the FA and the PO as they develop a support strategy. Although this tool is presented as a checklist, assessing a PO's capacity involves much more than ticking boxes: it is a long-term process that requires considerable sensitivity, skill, and experience.

As it is not possible for the FA or PO to address all capacity-development needs at the same time, both will have to prioritise areas for support at each stage of the support process. The following questions can help FAs prioritise support activities together with the PO:

- What objectives and whose interests are driving the support priorities identified by the PO?
- How important is the proposed support to different groups within the PO, e.g. to leaders, managers, and to male and female members?
- What type of support is most important for the PO's survival: generating short-term benefits to build members' commitment to the business or investing in long-term financial sustainability?
- Will the proposed support activity enable the PO to progress towards greater financial sustainability and organisational independence?
- Does the PO need to develop capacity in other areas before the investment in the proposed area will pay off?

Summary: initial steps and considerations

- Before initiating a support project, FAs need to assess whether certain minimum conditions in the market system and within existing POs are present, as this may have important implications for the approach and resources required to support POs effectively.
- A rapid market and producer assessment, conducted by specialists, provides an important foundation for planning and prioritising PO support activities.
- Where possible FAs should try to support existing POs rather than forming new POs, as this is a challenging process and may not lead to sustainable organisations.
- A potential gender and poverty impact assessment can help FAs assess gaps in their planned work with POs and identify what complementary support activities may be necessary.
- FAs need to plan all their work with POs with a clear exit strategy agreed with the PO.

- FAs need to assess their own support capacity and organisational commitment to the support project before beginning their work, to avoid changes in strategy that may disrupt POs' development.
- Support provided to POs should, ideally, be based on a mutually agreed support strategy that is explained in a service contract or memorandum of understanding between the FA and PO and is based on a joint assessment of the PO's development needs and priorities.

14 | Facilitating the producer organisation support process

The aim of this chapter is to provide an overview of the main support priorities and issues in each of the eight areas of PO capacity shown in Figure 14.1.

Many of the issues discussed in the following eight sections are relevant to both new and more advanced POs. More detailed guidance on supporting more advanced PO activities, such as processing and advocacy, is provided in Chapter 15, while Chapter 16 looks at the process of forming new POs.

As these eight areas are interconnected, it is not possible to provide a simple plan on how and in which order to work on each of these issues. This will depend on the needs and priorities of the PO and the capacity of the FA and other service providers. Based on the information in each section FAs should be able to:

- identify the core capacities POs need to develop in each of these eight areas;
- understand some of the main development issues and challenges in relation to each area;

Figure 14.1: Eight areas of producer organisation capacity

Empowering Grassroots Members (14.1)	Strengthening Governance and Leadership (14.2)	Supporting Effective Market Research (14.3)	Strengthening Business Management (14.4)
Supporting Improved Production (14.5)	Supporting Appropriate PO Structures (14.6)	Facilitating Trade Linkages (14.7)	Facilitating Access to Market Services (14.8)

- draw on examples of good practice and innovative approaches in each area;
- identify where the FA will need to bring in support from specialists or mobilise additional resources.

14.1 Empowering grassroots members

We start this chapter by looking at the capacity-development needs of individual grassroots members. It is easy for FAs to focus their support on leaders and managers, as they are usually the first and main contact point for FAs. However, POs can only become successful producer-owned and producer-controlled businesses if individual members have the capacity to exercise ownership and control over the business. Table 14.1 identifies four factors that affect whether members exercise this ownership and control.

We will look at capacity and cultural norms in this section, with a particular focus on gender attitudes and empowering women to participate in POs. We will deal with formal structures and rules, and motivation and trust in the following sections.

Table 14.1: Factors affecting whether members exercise ownership and control over the PO

Capacity	Individual members need to have the knowledge, skills, time, and confidence to exercise their rights and participate in decision-making processes. For example, members may be illiterate and therefore unable to read internal reports or future plans presented by the leadership.
Cultural norms	Cultural norms and expectations may constrain members' ability to use their skills and exercise their right to participate in decision-making. For example, women may not be expected to participate in decision-making processes or to take on leadership roles.
Formal structures and rules	These define members' rights and the formal systems of decision-making and control, such as voting rights, for example.
Motivation and trust	If individual members do not trust the PO's decision-making process or they are not satisfied with the benefits they receive from the PO they may become disillusioned and withdraw from active involvement in the PO.

Members' capacity to exercise ownership and control

FAs can help POs develop their capacity to exercise ownership and control in the following key areas:

- *Basic numeracy and literacy:* a lack of basic numeracy and literacy can limit producers' confidence and ability to participate in the PO's affairs. Women, in particular, often lack literacy and numeracy skills. For example, in its work in sub-Saharan Africa, CLUSA provides training to develop PO members' functional literacy and numeracy skills, before developing business and marketing skills. This approach draws on Paulo Freire's use of literacy to help villagers define their own development priorities.[41]

- *Business and market literacy:*[42] PO members need to have a basic understanding of markets and their business if they are to participate meaningfully in discussions and decisions about the PO's activities and ensure that the PO's managers are acting in their interest. Specialist support agencies have developed various participatory methodologies, such as participatory market mapping, to help producers develop this basic understanding.

- *Building confidence:* a lack of confidence can prevent members, especially women, from participating in decision-making and contributing their knowledge and insights to the PO. The very process of participating in a collective marketing activity is likely to increase the confidence of many members, but some members, and particularly women, may need further support, especially if cultural norms dictate that women should not participate in this way. One way to build confidence is to give members the opportunity to visit other producers in a different context and see with their own eyes how other producers have overcome similar challenges.

- *Changing business attitudes:* members' sense of ownership and initiative can be weakened by unhealthy attitudes towards the business. Such attitudes might include the expectation that the FA will solve all business problems, or a continued focus on production rather than on the demands of the market. These attitudes are often deep-seated and FAs will need to work with POs to encourage attitudes that will support and sustain the POs' business. In Mozambique, for example, Oxfam GB hired a specialist agency to conduct a participatory internal assessment with a PO to help its members reflect on their organisation and members' attitudes towards the organisation. As a result members and leaders identified weaknesses within the organisation and developed a strategy to improve grassroots ownership of the PO.

- *Basic management and accounting skills:* management and accounting training is normally provided only to existing leaders and managers, as it is too expensive to provide such training to ordinary members. As a result, most ordinary members and especially women do not have the opportunity to develop the skills necessary to become a leader, and existing leaders may therefore consolidate their position of power. Of course, in large POs it is impossible to provide such training to more than a handful of members but FAs need to balance the costs of providing such training to additional members against the benefits of greater grassroots ownership and control.

Influencing gender attitudes

Although FAs can sometimes push POs to adopt certain rules or structures which increase the participation of women, for example by introducing a quota for women in leadership positions, this may do little to change underlying attitudes and can even make life more difficult for the women in question. Unless there is a gradual change in the attitudes towards women and the division of labour within the household, there may be very little real change, even if POs can point to the one or two women represented on their board. To support real change in women's ability to participate equally in POs, FAs need to develop an in-depth understanding of the capacity, needs, and priorities of women within local communities and the PO. Change will often take considerable time and FAs need to engage in a dialogue with PO leaders about the investments and changes that are needed to increase women's participation in the PO. FAs may consider one of the following strategies to facilitate real change:

- *Targeted support:* targeting specific support at women or other marginalised groups that are disadvantaged and excluded. For example, in the Dominican Republic, Oxfam GB provided leadership training for women, and resources to enable women to meet together and discuss their problems.
- *Promoting greater involvement of both husbands and wives:* in Albania, for example, men were encouraged to participate in and support their wives in their collective bee-keeping initiative. As a result the group and their initiative have contributed to real change within the households as men have begun to take on some domestic work to enable their wives to concentrate on bee-keeping.
- *Women-only POs:* women may need to form their own POs or create separate first-level organisations within a larger PO to feel comfortable participating in the PO and voicing their opinions. In the short to medium term, this strategy may provide the only way for

women to participate freely within a PO although women may benefit more, in the long term, if the underlying problems that prevent them from participating on an equal basis in mixed groups are addressed.
- *Building on trust:* in some cultures women are more trusted with managing money than men and FAs can help women make the most of this advantage by encouraging POs to give women more responsibility in managing finances and by providing accountancy training specifically for women.

Summary: empowering grassroots members

- Increasing members' ability to exercise ownership and control of the PO depends on their capacity, local cultural norms, the formal rules and structure of the PO, and members' motivation and trust.
- FAs can support the empowerment of grassroots members by developing their skills in critical areas, including numeracy and literacy, and business and market literacy, as well as building members' confidence, for example through exchanges with other POs.
- Promoting equal participation of women in POs requires particular attention to underlying gender attitudes that affect women's opportunities and the division of labour within the home and on the farm; thereby constraining women's time, resources, and confidence to participate in POs.

14.2 Strengthening governance and leadership

Helping to strengthen POs' governance and leadership involves support and investment in many different areas. This section focuses on three critical areas for FAs' support.

Formal structures and rules

As we noted in the previous chapter, formal structures and rules are one important factor that determine members' ability to participate in decision-making and exercise their ownership of the PO. As POs develop, these structures and rules will need to be formalised in a constitution that is approved by the membership and which sets out the PO's vision and mission, and the formal structures and rules of governance and decision-making.

In many cases, the formal structures and rules of POs give all members the right to participate on an equal basis within the PO, but members' actual ability to exercise these rights is constrained by cultural norms or a lack of capacity. However, changes in the formal structures and rules are sometimes necessary and can make a difference as the following examples show:

- *Membership rules:* changing the rules to extend membership to spouses enabled women to participate more actively in the PO Fedecares, in the Dominican Republic.
- *Voting system:* voting in many POs is conducted by a show of hands, which can constrain the ability of women and other marginalised members to vote freely, and can consolidate the power of the leadership. Introducing a secret voting system can help to change this.
- *Political office:* to avoid conflict of interests POs may not permit elected leaders to hold any form of political office. This can prevent unwelcome interference in the management of the PO and also prevent already powerful members from consolidating their position within the PO. NASFAM introduced such a rule from the start, which has enabled it to avoid many of the political entanglements that often affect co-operatives in Malawi.
- *Disciplinary procedures:* to encourage transparent behaviour and prevent the loss of trust that can weaken the organisation, POs should be encouraged to establish clear rules governing the behaviour of members, leaders, and managers, including effective monitoring systems and disciplinary procedures.
- *Quotas:* one way of encouraging more representative leadership within POs is to introduce a formal quota, which makes it a requirement for each level of the organisation to involve a minimum number of women leaders. However, formal quotas alone do little to change attitudes towards women and the division of labour within the home that can prevent women from participating in POs. NASFAM, for example, only applies a formal quota on women's representation at the AGM and instead encourages greater participation through leadership training and competitions that reward clubs and associations in which women are most active.
- *Leadership rotation:* POs need to find the right balance between leadership continuity, ensuring effective management; and leadership rotation, an important function of accountability and grassroots control. Most PO constitutions require leadership rotation by limiting the number of years that leaders can hold their position. However, it is not uncommon for leaders to remain in their position for much longer, as in the example of UFP, which we discussed in Chapter 7. Although FAs can sometimes use their position to force PO leaders to stand down once they have completed their term in office, such

interventions undermine POs' independence and can destabilise the organisation. A more effective approach can be for FAs to invest in leadership training for potential new leaders, while encouraging leaders to recognise the benefits of leadership rotation by organising exchange visits with POs where this is common practice.

Although constitutions and their rules are important, they have little value if they are not owned and understood by PO members. FAs may need to work with PO leaders and grassroots members to make the constitution a document that is understood and owned by members and enables them to exercise their rights and responsibilities within the organisation.

Social capital

Formal structures and rules are important but effective governance and leadership depends as much, if not more, on the level of social capital within the PO. In Chapters 3 and 7, we emphasised the important role that trust and commitment among members and trust in the leadership play in the governance of POs. The example of Kuapa Kokoo, the cocoa co-operative in Ghana, underlines the importance of social capital in developing a strong business. Initially, the co-operative faced considerable problems and a major crisis as it had to borrow money at high interest rates to pay its members for their cocoa, and buyers did not pay the co-operative until much later. However, after a few years, members had developed sufficient trust and confidence in the co-operative that they were willing to deliver their cocoa without immediate payment. This 'deferred payment system' meant that the co-operative no longer had to borrow money to pay its members.

Social capital within POs depends on many things, including the extent to which members share a common identity or background, and the frequency of communication and interaction between the members of the group. Here we will briefly consider what role FAs can play to help build social capital within POs:

- *Improving communication:* good internal communication within groups and between different levels of the PO is critical and has to be adapted to the needs and capacity of members. Written communication is often inappropriate if only a few members can read, and more time and resources may be needed to allow regular open meetings. NASFAM, for example, has invested in various forms of communication, including notice boards at its farm supply shops, a quarterly magazine, and monthly radio broadcasts, which are all part-funded by grants from donors.

- *Tolerating homogeneity:* FAs may be tempted to push for more inclusive POs that are more representative of the local community. However, as we suggested above, PO success often depends on the level of trust and understanding among members and so FAs should avoid pushing for greater diversity within POs. As we saw in Case Study 9, large differences between individual members' contributions and capacity can create significant tensions within POs.

- *Supporting women's groups:* research shows that women's groups are often better than mixed or male groups at managing joint assets, and women's groups often develop a high level of social capital, despite other differences between group members.[43] Encouraging separate first-level organisations for women therefore often makes good business sense – NASFAM, for example, has many women-only clubs.
- *Supporting regular interactions:* encouraging group members to meet on a regular basis, even when there is no group business to be conducted, is also important. This can be difficult when the business revolves around a short harvest or when members invest in perennial crops that take a number of years before they yield a harvest. In this case FAs may be able to support the development of the group through complementary activities aimed at bringing members together on a regular basis.
- *Promoting organic growth:* as we saw in the case of UFP in Chapter 7, POs that expand very quickly often face difficulties maintaining social capital across the organisation. It is important to keep this in mind as FAs sometimes encourage rapid growth in order to meet their own or donors' project targets. FAs can play an important role in helping POs to grow organically and by discouraging over-ambitious leaders from expanding too rapidly.

Leadership

Strong leadership is critical to the success of any PO and can help smooth tensions and build trust and confidence among members. Conversely, weak leadership and leadership problems are a common cause of PO failure and it is therefore important for FAs to help develop the capacity of leaders. For example, in Uganda, many coffee co-operatives collapsed in the 1990s due to the impact of liberalisation, but in many cases bad management and dishonest leaders were as much to blame. There are three main areas of leadership capacity that FAs need to consider:

- *Management skills:* such skills are often taught through traditional training workshops but FAs should also consider experience-based learning methods, such as exposure visits, action learning, mentoring, or secondments. Such methodologies are particularly important to help leaders develop more advanced management skills, such as the ability to analyse the strengths and weaknesses of the organisation, manage change, resolve conflict, and articulate a vision and mission for the organisation.

- *Business understanding:* as we discussed in Chapter 7, elected leaders need to have the capacity to monitor and control the performance of professional managers. To perform this role effectively, elected leaders need to develop more than just a superficial understanding of the business and market systems. However, this is often difficult to reconcile with regular leadership rotation, as it is impossible to train every newly elected leader. There are two ways to overcome or reduce this problem: firstly, POs may appoint non-executive leaders from outside the organisation who have the necessary experience. Four of NASFAM's 12 board members, for example, are invited from outside the PO, based on their technical or commercial experience. Secondly, POs may organise leadership elections to ensure that leaders' terms in office do not run in parallel and there are always more experienced leaders to support newly elected leaders. FAs can encourage such strategies where appropriate and support additional business training where necessary.

- *Integrity and dedication:* ultimately, effective governance depends on the integrity of leaders and their dedication to the task. These virtues have to be promoted from within the PO, that is, by the attitudes of individual members and leaders and the rules governing leaders' accountability and behaviour. Where necessary, FAs may be able to help POs develop appropriate rules and controls to promote more accountable and transparent leadership. The rules on leaders' allowances and expenses may be particularly important as they may affect whether being a leader is seen as a privileged responsibility and duty, for which leaders receive compensation, or as an opportunity for personal gain.

Summary: strengthening governance and leadership

- The formal rules and structure of POs are important and can affect decision-making and participation within the PO, but unless members understand these rules and have the ability and motivation to participate in decision-making, these rules and structures may be of little value.
- Social capital is the glue that keeps POs together. Social capital can be built over time and depends on a shared identity or background, frequent interaction, good communication, and effective leadership.
- Strong leadership is essential for the effective governance of POs, and FAs can help to improve leadership capacity by developing management skills and business understanding.

14.3 Supporting effective market research

To compete in the market, POs have to base their production and marketing activities on the demands of the target market. Effective business planning should therefore start with an assessment of the market system and the identification of viable market opportunities.

FAs can play an important role facilitating market research and helping POs develop a realistic marketing strategy, but the desire to see immediate results can tempt FAs to conduct their own market research or hire a consultant to do the work and then present the best market options to the PO. Such support can make life easier for a PO in the short term but in the long term POs have to develop the skills to conduct or manage market research themselves. As we saw in Case Study 10, Aprainores faced considerable difficulties when it suddenly had to conduct market research and identify new markets for the first time. FAs may therefore not help POs in the long run by providing such assistance, not least because PO members may lose an important opportunity to meet buyers or consumers face to face, and understand their needs and expectations. Market research and identifying viable marketing options requires expertise and so most FAs will need to help POs access appropriate support and services from specialists. The further reading and resources section in Annex 1 lists various guides and manuals that provide detailed guidance on how to conduct participatory market research.

Market research

Table 14.2 summarises some of the main steps involved in market research.

Although FAs should ideally help facilitate the PO's market research, FAs often face the problem that donors expect funding proposals to be based on market analysis to justify the application for funding. Where possible, FAs should aim to involve POs in this initial research and should also earmark funds within the funding proposal to facilitate the PO's own research, even where this may duplicate earlier research, as it represents an important learning process for POs. Once the information has been collected, POs need to analyse the information and identify a small number of realistic marketing options.

Table 14.2: Main steps of market research

Market research steps	Comments
Analysing existing products and markets	POs can learn important lessons from an assessment of their past marketing activities.
Planning research	FAs may need to help POs decide: • Whether they have the skills and capacity to conduct the research themselves or whether they need to hire experts. • Whether they can conduct the research alongside an expert to learn the necessary skills at the same time. • What resources are required to conduct the research themselves (e.g. travel) or to hire experts to conduct the research? In new or small POs it may sometimes be useful to involve some grassroots members in market research in order to develop market literacy and promote a market-oriented approach.
Conducting or managing the research	PO staff may need basic training in marketing and market research in order to conduct their own research or to manage the specialist providing the service for them. Existing information on markets collected by government agencies or other organisations can be very useful, if it is available and accurate, especially for more distant markets.

Developing a marketing strategy

Once a PO has identified a small number of market options, it needs to develop a marketing strategy based on a careful assessment of the options and the PO members' priorities and capacity. This assessment should narrow down the options to two or three marketing options, covering different markets, different products, or a combination of both. The following issues should be considered in this process:

- *Members' priorities:* the PO members' priorities, in terms of their business and social objectives and the balance between risk and profitability, have to be reflected in the final short-list.
- *Competitive advantage:* unless the PO can sell a product at a lower price than other producers (and still offer its members a sustainable income), or offer a better product that justifies a higher price, it will struggle to compete.

- *Market risk:* POs need to pay particular attention to the risk involved in different marketing options. The most profitable opportunities are often the most risky and so POs need to find the right balance between security and profitability for their members. Figure 14.2 provides a simple method of assessing the risk of different marketing strategies. According to this matrix, marketing risk increases from 1 to 4 with each of the product and market combinations.
- *PO capacity:* where POs have a choice between domestic or export markets, a good rule is for POs to first gain experience and develop their capacity in the domestic market before attempting to access more risky and demanding export markets. Agrolempa's experience demonstrates that a combination of domestic markets may offer good business with lower risks (Case Study 1).
- *Non-monetised costs:* in rural economies production and processing are often dependent on 'free' family labour or exchanged labour from other community members. Some market options may involve crop choices that have important implications for natural resources or a household's ability to produce other crops. All these options involve costs that are rarely considered in cash value even though they affect the livelihoods of family members, in particular women. These costs need to be taken into account when POs assess different market options. For example, crops that demand a lot of water can reduce water availability for staple food crops required for domestic consumption.

It is a good idea to test the final options through a more detailed feasibility study or a pilot marketing project, and FAs may need to help POs finance such a study. The final choice of marketing options then needs to be outlined in a marketing strategy, which can be very simple or more complex, depending on the nature of the marketing activity and the capacity of the PO.

Figure 14.2: Ansoff Matrix for assessing marketing risk[44]

	Existing Products	New Products
Existing Markets	1. Market Penetration	3. Product Development
New Markets	2. Market Development	4. Diversification

Facilitating the producer organisation support process | 111

How marketing strategies affect participation

In Chapter 4 we noted that a PO's choice of marketing strategy will often affect who can participate in the PO's activities. For example, poorer producers may not have the skills or assets required to produce high-value products. These producers might either be prevented from joining POs, remain members but receive few benefits, or be forced out of the PO because they cannot meet the minimum production requirements. However, in most cases POs will not be able to include such members, at least in the short term, without weakening their business or becoming donor-funded institutions rather than financially sustainable businesses.

FAs should mobilise their own and other actors' resources, including the government, to build the assets and develop the skills of poorer producers to meet the production and marketing requirements of the PO, which are ultimately dictated by the market. The following is a list of different measures FAs can adopt to support poorer producers:

- Implement complementary development projects that build the capacity of poorer small-scale producers to participate in more demanding market or value chains. Such projects may focus on developing agricultural skills, improving irrigation, or building household assets to increase producers' capacity to take risks.

- Mobilise a campaign to lobby for government investments in infrastructure, land re-distribution, and market services to improve the production capacity of poor small-scale producers.

- Develop the capacity of large, established POs to support staple food marketing activities, which may open up participation to women in countries where most staples are produced by women. To compete in low-value staple markets, POs may have to invest in processing to add value and thereby access higher value markets. One of NASFAM's associations, for example, has invested in a rice-milling and packaging plant and now markets its own brand of rice to supermarkets in Malawi.

- Assist with organic or Fairtrade certification which, in some cases, may enable poorer producers to access less competitive markets with higher margins. However, the quality and food-safety demands of these markets will still pose major challenges for the poorest producers.

Summary: identifying marketing opportunities

- FAs should focus on helping POs to manage or conduct their own market research rather than organising research for POs and then presenting marketing options to them.

- In small and new POs, members' involvement in market research can help them understand the market and develop a market-oriented approach.
- FAs can help POs develop a marketing strategy that reflects members' priorities and willingness to take risks and the PO's competitive advantage and capacity.
- Certain market opportunities may create increased non-monetised costs, which should be assessed during the market appraisal.
- The choice of markets and marketing strategy will affect who can participate in PO activities and FAs may need to implement complementary development activities or mobilise government investments to ensure that poorer producers and women have the opportunities and capacity to participate in POs.

14.4 Strengthening business management

Managing a PO business involves managing people, finances, facilities, operations, and different management activities including planning, organising, and monitoring. To manage these effectively requires considerable skills and experience, which is why many POs hire professional managers if they can afford it. Developing this management capacity requires specialist expertise and few FAs will have the necessary skills and experience to provide direct support to POs in this area. However, FAs can play an important role in linking POs to specialists and addressing short-term financing gaps. In this section we will focus on financial management, as this often presents the greatest challenge to POs, their managers, and leaders.

Business planning

Business planning is essential for POs to compete in the market, to become financially sustainable, and to deliver real benefits to their members. A core focus of business planning is developing a business strategy that will deliver these objectives (see Chapter 8 for practical examples). Developing a viable strategy demands skills and experience and PO managers may require considerable training and support to develop these skills, especially if they have to rely on existing members to manage the business. Although it is not practical for all PO members to be involved in the business-planning process, as the owners of the business, members should be consulted about significant changes and required to approve new plans to ensure their interests are taken into account.

Business planning is not primarily about writing a business plan although the business plan is an important document. The important thing is the process of analysing the business and its markets, developing individual understanding of and gaining broad agreement on a viable business strategy, and setting clear targets and objectives. This process brings together many of the activities described in the different sections of this chapter. A business-planning process and plan should ideally include the following steps:

1. Agreeing the overall goal and objectives of the PO for a defined period of time (e.g. 3–5 years) based on members' priorities and an analysis of the PO's strengths and weaknesses and development priorities.
2. An analysis of the target market based on previous market research (see 14.3).
3. An assessment of the market services the PO needs in order to conduct and develop its business and an assessment of what market services are available in the area (see 14.7).
4. An assessment of current and potential constraints within the market environment.
5. A business strategy or 'business model' that explains how the PO will compete in the market and become profitable over the agreed time period. This strategy should be based on identified market opportunities, the marketing strategy, and the PO's priorities and capacity.
6. A financial plan that provides a detailed analysis of expected income, outgoings, profitability, and cash flow.

Analysing business costs

POs often fail because they are unable to cover all their costs with their business income. Although most businesses take some years before they break even and become profitable, some POs are based on poor business strategies that will never generate sufficient income to cover their costs. FAs sometimes keep these POs above water by covering some of their costs while in reality the business is not sustainable. It is essential that FAs work with POs from the very start to avoid investing in business strategies that will ultimately fail.

FAs can help POs by linking them to business specialists who can analyse their business model and help the PO develop a viable business strategy. FAs can also help POs by encouraging a careful analysis of the PO's costs, including:

- *Running or overhead costs:* these include staff salaries and expenses and the cost of offices and office equipment.
- *Business service and development-support service costs:* these include hiring vehicles, financing market information and research services, and the cost of management training or accessing specialist advice.

- *Cost of borrowing:* raising funds for trading or investments involves a cost (e.g. bank interest) that, in the long term at least, has to be covered from business income.
- *Cost of PO services provided to members:* all the services the PO provides to members, including marketing, trading, extension, training, storage, etc., involve running costs and capital costs (such as vehicles or warehouses).

As POs frequently face difficulties raising funds, FAs often provide funding for running costs, large investments, and certain market services. If this funding is provided as a grant, POs may not even think of raising and repaying funds as a normal business cost. The danger is that these costs are not accounted for in the PO's business strategy and so its business is based on an unsustainable foundation. FAs should therefore cost their own support services and encourage POs to account for these costs in their business plan, even if the FA covers some or all of them during the first years of support. As a PO develops, the FA should begin to charge for a growing share of its support services, which also provides a useful indicator of how much the PO values the FA's services.

Cash-flow management

Even a very profitable PO will face severe difficulties if it runs out of cash and is unable to pay its clients or members. Kuapa Kokoo in Ghana almost collapsed because it did not have sufficient cash to buy cocoa from its members even though its business was profitable. Some NASFAM associations have lost business in the past because they were not able to pay members immediately and so some members sold their produce to local traders. Good cash-flow management is therefore essential, especially for POs engaged in agricultural activities where timing is often critical. FAs can help POs by developing the capacity of leaders and managers to manage the PO's cash flow, and by helping POs to access sufficient operational funds.

Financing and investment

Although small-scale producers usually have limited assets, a financial contribution to the business from members, however small, can increase their sense of ownership and represent a valuable indicator of the members' commitment to the PO. For this reason, it is important that POs expect a minimum contribution from their members in the form of membership fees and share purchases. Asprepatía's members, for example, contributed 23 per cent of the PO's initial operational fund (Case Study 8), while the Clam Clubs in Viet Nam raised all their start-up capital from members' investments (Case Study 2). To ensure that the poorer members of the community can invest in the Clam Clubs, Oxfam GB set up a revolving loan fund from which poor members can borrow money at a very low interest rate. FAs may need to consider implementing similar complementary activities to ensure membership fees or investment requirements do not exclude poorer producers.

Although members' contributions are important, most POs have to either borrow money, attract investors, or access grants to begin trading or fund larger investments. As banks are often reluctant to lend money to POs, and investors are only willing to invest if they can have some control over the business, POs frequently face significant problems raising the money they need. FAs can play a strategic role helping POs access funds, although FAs need to consider carefully how best to facilitate this. Table 14.3 outlines five ways FAs can help POs access financing.

Table 14.3: Different ways FAs can support POs' access to financing

Financing Support	Comment
Grant funding	One of the most common ways for FAs to finance POs is to provide a grant for operational funds, to provide investments, or to cover running costs. FAs may also broker grant funding from another donor. Grant funding is a simple solution in the short term but is not sustainable in the long term and should therefore be limited to specific, time-bound, phased contributions that are properly accounted for in the business strategy.
Linking POs to financial institutions	Introducing POs to a financial institution and, if necessary, helping them apply for a loan (without formally sponsoring their application) is a simple and sustainable strategy that FAs should pursue wherever possible.
Providing a guarantee	One reason POs often cannot access loans from banks is because they cannot offer any collateral. By providing a formal or informal guarantee, FAs can sometimes help POs access loans. However, if the bank is unwilling to make future loans without the FA's guarantee, this strategy is also not sustainable.
Providing a loan	Some FAs may have the capacity and systems to offer loans to POs either directly or through associated lending organisations. In many cases such loans are 'soft' loans, with much lower interest rates than those offered by commercial lenders.
Equity investments	In some cases, FAs may be able to raise funds for the PO's business by buying a share in the PO's business (i.e. equity), as in the case of OAPI (Case Study 7). However, according to our definition in Chapter 1, this should only be a temporary arrangement and the FA should gradually transfer its shares to the PO. This strategy involves considerable risks and should therefore only be considered in specific circumstances.

Each of the approaches to financing POs has advantages and disadvantages and FAs must try to find the right balance between helping POs access essential financing in the short term and encouraging POs to develop a sustainable business in the long term. Many POs will need long-term financial support to have a chance of developing into sustainable businesses; however, FAs need to provide this support in such a way as to minimise the tendency of external grants to weaken internal accountability, ownership, and initiative within the PO.

Summary: strengthening business management

- Business planning, including analysing the business and market systems and developing a realistic and sustainable business strategy, is essential for POs to become profitable and generate benefits for their members.
- Many POs fail because they do not analyse their business costs carefully, and their business strategy does not account for the costs of accessing market services or borrowing money, which in the long run have to be covered from business income.
- FAs need to help POs develop effective cash-flow management systems to ensure they can meet financial obligations to their members and service providers on a day-to-day basis.
- Wherever possible POs should try to raise some of their capital from members' contributions in order to increase their ownership and commitment to the business. FAs may need to provide assistance to poorer producers to ensure that they are not excluded on account of these contribution requirements.
- FAs can play a strategic role in helping POs to access funds for their business, but they should avoid financing POs in a way that weakens their long-term sustainability.

14.5 Supporting improved production

This section looks at how FAs can support POs to produce products that meet the demands of the market, in terms of quantity, quality, and continuity. We will consider processing in Chapter 15.

Co-ordinating production

Co-ordinating the production of individual members is important as it enables POs to:

- *Meet supply contracts:* POs often make advance contracts with buyers to supply a certain amount, and POs have to co-ordinate members' production to ensure they can fulfil the contract.

- *Increase the range and seasonal coverage of production:* by organising individual members to produce different products or to produce the same product at different times, POs can increase the range of products they can offer buyers and ensure a constant supply throughout the season.
- *Reduce business costs:* co-ordinating members' production can enable POs to use their resources more efficiently and reduce wastages.

FAs can help POs develop the logistical skills and systems to co-ordinate members' production to meet market demands. Some POs may engage in collective production where members produce products together, such as the collective clam-raising activity of the Clam Clubs. However, in the agricultural sector, collective production rarely offers advantages over individual production, as it requires higher management costs and can lead to 'free riding' by some members.

Increasing output

Most POs have to find ways to increase their total output, i.e. the total quantity they are able to market, in order to reduce their business costs (per unit sold), or to increase their bargaining power with buyers. POs can increase their output by:

- *Increasing the number of members:* Asprepatía, for example, increased its bargaining power by attracting new members.
- *Increasing the productivity of individual members:* NASFAM, for example, provides extension training and input services to members, and encourages competition between clubs, offering premiums and prizes (sponsored by companies) to the most productive groups.
- *Buying produce from non-members:* POs such as Agrolempa act as 'portal companies', buying produce from members and non-members to meet the quantities demanded by buyers.

FAs can play an important role helping POs to implement these strategies. This may involve supporting membership growth at a sustainable rate with the necessary investments in training new members and leaders. As few POs have the resources to fund extension services, and government extension services are often missing or weak, FAs can also help to mobilise the necessary services from government agencies, research centres, technical colleges, other NGOs, or private companies. FAs need to help POs pay particular attention to the training needs of different members and especially the different needs of men and women. Successful trading demands specialist skills and experience, and POs may need temporary financial assistance to pay for professional managers until the business has reached a profitable scale.

Quality management

Improving product quality is an important strategy for POs to access higher value markets and increase their bargaining power, as we saw in Chapter 8. Product quality depends on a range of subjective and objective criteria, including:[45]

- *Market acceptance:* the subjective preferences of consumers in terms of the product's appearance, taste, or nutritional value.
- *Health and safety:* these requirements are usually expressed in standards, covering the level of permitted pesticide residues on agricultural produce or additives in processed foods.
- *Consistency:* buyers want consistent quality so they do not have to check every item, and consumers often favour products that have a predictable quality.
- *Shelf-life:* many agricultural products deteriorate over time, and their quality therefore depends on transport and storage conditions and on how long it takes to get the product to the consumer.
- *Packaging and labelling:* packaging and labelling are considered an integral part of a product's quality in most export markets.

POs need to conduct market research to understand the preferences of buyers and consumers and the standards that their products have to meet. FAs can help POs meet buyers or exporters at trade fairs and commodity markets so that POs can discuss buyers' preferences and the relevant quality standards. Once the demands of the market are understood, POs may need to:

- develop the capacity of their members to improve the quality of their produce;
- create appropriate incentive systems that reward members for quality products;
- develop a quality-management system to ensure that the PO's produce meets the necessary standards and expectations.

POs will often need support to help their members improve product quality. FAs may be able to mobilise relevant market services and investments from the government, exporters, or other agencies to improve members' production techniques and productive assets. In some cases, FAs may decide to implement complementary projects aimed at improving members' production capacity.

Quality-management systems are often essential if POs want to access export markets or supply demanding local markets. These involve either quality control (testing the quality of finished products) or quality assurance (controlling and monitoring product quality at each stage of the production process). Both these approaches involve costs, including:

- *Monitoring costs:* POs may need to employ and train staff to monitor and control product quality or pay for laboratory tests.
- *Cost of product losses:* PO members may not be able to sell all their produce to the PO if it does not meet the required standards or if members have not followed the required production process.
- *Increased production costs:* individual members will often have to invest in improved technology or more labour-intensive production techniques to meet the required quality standards.

Developing an effective and efficient quality-control and assurance system is therefore no simple task and requires significant resources and commitment from all PO members. As few POs have the resources or access to financing to invest in quality-management systems, FAs can play an important role facilitating access to funds and to the specialists required to advise the PO and train its staff. Any financial assistance provided by FAs or other agencies needs to be based on a realistic assessment of how the PO will cover the running costs of a quality-management system in the long run from increased sales income.

Independent certification

Supermarkets and their suppliers usually require a PO's quality-management system to be approved by an independent agency to ensure it meets the necessary standard. The farmer co-operatives supplying OAPI, for example, were certified by an accredited agency to prove their products meet organic standards. To satisfy European Union food-safety standards, NASFAM had to send samples of its groundnuts to an accredited laboratory in South Africa to check aflatoxin levels, as there was no accredited agency in Malawi. The Fairtrade Labelling Organisation (FLO) also requires POs to be certified by FLO-Cert against FLO standards before they can sell products under the Fairtrade system. As with quality-management systems, certification usually involves considerable costs. Certification fees are often high and POs may have to develop internal management and monitoring systems so that the certifying agency can certify the whole PO without having to check each individual member, which can increase the costs dramatically.

POs often face difficulties accessing independent certification, as they do not have the funds to pay certification fees or lack the resources and expertise to invest in appropriate internal monitoring systems. For example, producers usually have to use organic methods for three years before they can obtain organic certification and sell products with an organic label. This conversion period can create problems for many POs as they may produce less during this period while also not receiving higher prices. Where certification is a key part of a PO's business strategy,

FAs can help POs overcome these challenges by facilitating access to specialists, mobilising funds for investments and fees from private companies or other agencies, and providing funds to help POs cover shortfalls during critical periods.

> **Summary: supporting improved production**
>
> - Co-ordinating members' production can enable POs to meet supply contracts and to satisfy buyers' demands, whilst lowering business costs. FAs may need to help POs develop the necessary logistical systems to co-ordinate production effectively.
> - POs have different options to increase their output, including increasing their membership, raising members' productivity, or buying produce from non-members. Each option requires additional skills and resources, which FAs may need to support.
> - Improving product quality is essential for POs to access better prices, but it involves a range of different costs, including the costs of extension services, quality-management systems, and certification, that POs are often unable to cover. FAs may be able to support such investment, providing that POs can realistically cover these costs in the long run from increased sales income, according to their business plan.

14.6 Supporting appropriate producer organisation structures

This section considers what role FAs can play to help POs develop a structure that fits their needs, priorities, and capacity.

Legal structure

In Chapter 6, we emphasised that there is no ideal legal structure and that POs need to adopt a legal structure that best fits their business needs and organisational priorities. FAs can assist POs in this decision by helping them to:

- access advice from local legal experts;
- consider the potential implications of different options, including both short-term and long-term advantages and disadvantages;
- negotiate the actual registration process.

FAs often expect POs to be legally registered before they provide any assistance. However, as we saw in Chapter 6, when POs are competing in informal markets, formal registration can create significant disadvantages and FAs should avoid pushing POs to register where this may weaken their business. Annex 4 provides an overview of the five legal structures introduced in Chapter 6 and shows how each deals with a range of important issues.

In some countries the laws governing collective businesses do not provide options that are suitable for POs, and the registration process is sometimes costly and bureaucratic. Furthermore, governments sometimes use laws to maintain control or influence over POs that weakens their independence. FAs can play an important role helping POs and other organisations to influence and change the laws so that POs can operate in a more favourable environment. Particular attention may need to be given to the rights of women to participate in existing or new proposed legal structures and their ability to form women-only organisations. Different legal structures may also assign membership and voting rights either to named individuals or to a household, which may have important implications both for women's participation and for the rights of other family members when a PO member dies.

For larger POs such as Agrolempa, mixed structures that involve a separate PO-owned trading or processing company often provide an ideal means of separating business management and organisational governance, and should be considered carefully, particularly as a PO's business develops (see Case Study 1 and section on mixed structures in Chapter 6).

Supporting producer organisation growth

PO expansion into a multi-level organisation is often essential to achieve the economies of scale required to become profitable and to increase bargaining power and influence in the market. However, expansion sometimes occurs without a careful analysis of the real costs of growth. Most of UFPs' second-level associations, for example, were set up with considerable financial support from donors and many now face difficulties trying to cover their running costs from their own income. Sometimes, growth can also be driven by FAs and their support projects rather than the initiative and needs of members. This is what happened with some of UCASN's second-level organisations as we saw in Chapter 7. Sustainable growth depends on the following factors:

- *Financing:* growth usually involves additional costs, as new structures require new staff, offices, and running costs. Unless the expanded structure enables the PO to cover these additional costs by generating additional business income, the PO's growth will not be financially sustainable. Although it can be tempting to finance PO expansion, FAs should avoid offering financial support for new structures unless POs have a realistic plan to cover all running costs from business income, within a clear timeframe. FAs should instead encourage

growth and expansion that is driven by the PO's business strategy and is based on a detailed analysis of the scale of activities necessary to break even.
- *Management capacity:* existing leaders and managers need to have the capacity to manage and control an expanded business, otherwise growth can lead to inefficient management and rising costs without significant gains.
- *Social capital:* social capital can be lost if POs grow too quickly and without grassroots support and ownership.

FAs should avoid offering incentives and resources that enable POs to grow faster than the organisation and business can support, given the existing level of management capacity and social capital. Instead FAs should help PO leaders and managers think through these issues and pursue a sustainable path based on a careful analysis of the costs and benefits of growth.

Summary: supporting appropriate PO structure

- FAs can help POs access the necessary legal advice to identify the most suitable legal structure for their business and organisation.
- FAs can also play an important role lobbying for an improved legal framework and registration process to ensure POs can compete on an equal basis with other businesses.
- FAs need to support organic and financially sustainable PO growth that is driven by the PO's business needs and its members' priorities.

14.7 Facilitating trade linkages

Unless POs have the resources to hire professional managers with commercial experience, they may lack the expertise to find buyers and negotiate sales. Although FA staff usually have little, if any, commercial experience, they may nonetheless have the contacts and reputation to identify buyers and negotiate sales on behalf of the PO. For example, in Mozambique a development NGO has negotiated supply contracts for chilli peppers with an exporter on behalf of the PO it is supporting. Table 14.4 identifies four different roles that FAs can play in facilitating PO's trade linkages.

Table 14.4: FA market linkage roles

FA role	Explanation
Trade partner	As a trade partner the FA buys produce from the PO and then sells it on to further buyers or directly to consumers. For example, until 2002, Oxfam GB used to import cashew nuts from Aprainores and sell them to consumers through its shops in the UK.
Broker	As a broker the FA finds buyers and negotiates contracts on behalf of the PO. PO staff may be involved in the process but are not the main actors. FAs may provide a formal guarantee to the buyer that the contract will be honoured. In the chilli pepper example above, the development NGO in Mozambique played the role of a broker on behalf of the PO.
Co-ordinator	As a co-ordinator the FA introduces the PO to buyers and may facilitate negotiation between the parties, but the PO has to do the actual negotiation. However, the FA's involvement and presence creates confidence and builds trust between the PO and potential buyers. In St Lucia, for example, Oxfam GB facilitated and developed relationships between four POs, potential buyers in the hotel sector, and other market actors, to promote dialogue and build trust between the different actors in the chain.
Adviser	As an adviser the FA provides guidance to the PO, either directly or through hired experts, but the PO has to find buyers and negotiate contracts independently and rely on its own reputation and credibility.

Few FAs have the capacity or networks to act as a trade partner or broker for POs. However, even when FA staff have the necessary skills and contacts they should think carefully before taking on such a role. As a broker the FA can help new or weak POs access better deals thereby generating immediate benefits, which may give the PO time to establish itself and build the commitment of its members. But acting as a broker can also encourage dependency on the FA and lead to unsustainable marketing arrangements, especially if buyers only agree to do business with POs because of guarantees provided by the FA. In Mozambique, for example, an exporter was unwilling to negotiate sales contracts directly with a PO even after repeated business transactions and would only deal with the international NGO working with the PO. Acting as a broker for POs can also weaken members' sense of ownership and initiative as they come to believe that the FA will resolve problems for them. FAs should therefore avoid acting as a broker or trading partner, except for a limited period of time and when a clear exit strategy has been agreed with the PO and the buyer. This exit strategy should involve considerable investment in the PO's staff to ensure that they develop the necessary skills and confidence to take over the FA's role. Where possible, FAs should instead focus on acting as a co-ordinator and adviser for POs' trade linkages.

Whatever their role, FAs need to invest in the capacity of POs to identify buyers and negotiate sales. Ultimately, POs need bargaining power to negotiate good deals; but to take full advantage of any bargaining power, POs need to develop capacity in the following areas:

- *Business understanding and judgement:* FAs can help PO staff to develop this understanding and judgement through formal business training but also by organising exposure or exchange visits to other businesses or POs. Particular attention may need to be given to ensure that women are able to participate in such activities. Oxfam GB, for example, organised exposure visits to markets and other clam businesses for the leaders of the Clam Clubs to help them gain a better understanding of the clam business.

- *Negotiation skills and confidence:* basic negotiation strategies can be taught, but real skills and confidence are only acquired through practical experience and working alongside experienced professionals. FAs can support such learning, for example, by seconding staff to work with experienced managers in other POs or businesses, or by hiring an experienced manager to work alongside staff in their day-to-day work. Again, special consideration should be given to ensure that women can also benefit from such initiatives.

- *Market information:* to negotiate effectively, POs need to have access to up-to-date information on market prices and conditions. We will look at market information services in the next section.

- *Reputation:* unless POs develop a good reputation as a reliable supplier they will struggle to find buyers or negotiate favourable sales contracts. POs will gain a bad reputation with buyers if they are unable to meet specific demands for quality or consistency or if PO members sell their products to other traders and the PO is therefore unable to meet existing sales agreements. FAs can help POs develop a good reputation by helping the PO to build trust and ownership among its grassroots members and by investing in members' production capacity and understanding of markets and its business.

Some of the guides and manuals listed in Annex 1 provide detailed guidance for POs and FAs on how to negotiate trade linkages, in particular between POs and commercial companies.

Summary: facilitating trade linkages

- FAs can facilitate POs' trade by acting as a trade partner, brokering sales on behalf of the PO, co-ordinating trade linkages between POs and buyers, or advising POs on their trade linkages.
- The challenge for FAs is to facilitate trade linkages in a way that does not weaken ownership within the PO and that helps the PO develop independent capacity to negotiate sales and develop a good reputation with buyers.

14.8 Facilitating access to market services

Access to appropriate market services is critical for POs to conduct and develop their business. FAs need to think carefully about what strategic role they can play in helping POs access these market services on a sustainable basis.

The first step is to help POs assess the market services they need to conduct and develop their business over the coming years. Once these have been identified, the next step is to assess what market services are available in the local area and wider region. This analysis should also assess whether service providers have experience of working with POs and small-scale producers and on what terms these services are offered (e.g. are they 'free' services offered by government departments or 'embedded services' offered by exporters as part of a sales contract). Usually this assessment should be conducted as part of the business-planning process described in 14.4.

Facilitating agency role and approach

As there are often many gaps in the market services available, and many services are unaffordable or not adapted to the needs of POs, FAs often rush to provide market services directly to POs without carefully considering the sustainability of their approach. Particularly, in thin and remote rural markets, where there are virtually no market service providers, FAs may fall into the role of primary market service provider without considering the long-term sustainability of these activities. The challenge for FAs is to determine whether it will be possible to link the PO to existing or new independent market service providers in the medium to long term or whether more fundamental constraints will prevent new service providers emerging without more significant state interventions and investments. Table 14.5 identifies four different roles FAs can play in helping POs access the necessary services.

Table 14.5: FA roles in facilitating access to market services

FA Role	Explanation
Market service provider	The FA provides market services directly to POs, using its own resources. In Viet Nam, Oxfam GB staff provided business training to the leaders of the Clam Clubs.
Market service manager	As a service manager, the FA identifies the service providers, manages service contracts on behalf of the PO, and pays for service costs. In Albania, for example, Oxfam GB identified and hired a wine specialist to advise the co-operative Zadrima.
Market service co-ordinator	As service co-ordinator, the FA may help the PO identify market service providers but the PO agrees the service contract and pays for part or all of the market service costs. The FA may act as a mediator between the PO and service provider to ensure the providers' services are adapted to the needs of the PO and its members. In India, Oxfam GB mediated between a commercial service provider and a new PO, as the service provider had no experience of working with small-scale producers.
Market service developer or mobiliser	If some important market services are not available in the local area, FAs may act as service developer to invest in the capacity of new or existing service providers to offer these services. FAs may also work with the PO and other organisations to lobby the government to provide these market services or offer incentives for private companies to provide these services. Where appropriate, FAs may also help POs develop the capacity to provide these market services themselves.

FAs can play a strategic role as service provider, especially where they have the necessary expertise to provide specific market services that are not otherwise available. However, FAs should always pay careful attention to the sustainability of their role and avoid providing market services directly unless a realistic and sustainable strategy is in place to hand over service provision to independent providers in the future. To become sustainable businesses in the long run POs have to be able to:

- access the necessary market services;
- pay for essential market services;
- identify and negotiate service contracts with any type of service provider.

Whatever role FAs play in the short term, they need to ensure these three conditions are met in the long run and this means focusing their attention on the service co-ordinator, service developer, or mobiliser role wherever possible.

Summary: facilitating access to market services

- Sustainable access to market services is essential for POs to conduct and develop their business, and FAs can help POs assess the market services they need and what market services are available.
- FAs can facilitate PO access to market services in various ways, including providing services directly, managing POs' access to services, co-ordinating POs' independent linkages to service providers, or developing the capacity of service providers.
- Whatever role FAs play, their aim should be to develop the capacity of POs to access, pay for, and negotiate contracts with service providers in the long term.

15 | Supporting advanced producer organisation activities

This chapter briefly considers three advanced PO activities:
- processing
- creating a brand
- advocacy

We refer to these as advanced activities because POs usually require a certain level of capacity to perform them successfully. For each, we will highlight some of the main challenges POs face in performing these activities before considering what role FAs can play in helping POs manage these activities effectively.

Processing

In Chapter 8, we noted that processing enables POs to add value to their product and to avoid potentially exploitative buyers in the market for unprocessed products. The vine growers' co-operative in Albania, for example, processes members' grapes to make wine which it can sell at a much higher price in the local market. OAPI, in India, buys and processes members' seed cotton in order to cut out exploitative traders in the local market and sell processed cotton directly to the weaving industry. Processing can therefore offer real benefits to producers but also involves considerable challenges that POs need to consider carefully:

- *Minimum scale:* investing in processing equipment or using independent processing services (i.e. sub-contracting) is usually only profitable above a certain minimum scale of activity. For example, Aprainores in El Salvador invested in a large nut-processing plant, but initially the members could only supply around a third of the quantity of nuts needed to operate the plant at full capacity, lower the operating costs, and make the processing activity competitive. To achieve the necessary scale, POs may need to expand their membership or buy produce from non-members, which will increase their costs and maybe also their business risks.

- *Business risk:* processing involves considerable risks, especially if the PO invests in its own processing equipment. Processing equipment is often expensive and has to be used efficiently to reduce costs and ensure the PO is competitive. In most cases, the equipment cannot be used for other purposes, which makes the business vulnerable to changes in the market and may weaken the PO's bargaining power.
- *Financing:* accessing affordable finance to pay for investments in processing equipment is a major difficulty for POs as we noted in the previous chapter. FAs and other donors can overcome this problem by offering grants or guarantees for such investments. However, grants can weaken the PO's sense of ownership of the initiative and, without the need to repay a loan or interest on the investment, the PO may not have the commercial discipline to use the equipment as efficiently and effectively as possible.
- *Management capacity:* managing a processing business is much more challenging and complex than simply collecting and marketing a commodity, and POs require considerably more management capacity to manage such a project successfully. Most POs will have to hire professional managers to ensure the business is managed effectively, but PO members still have to manage the managers, which also requires skill and understanding.
- *Structure:* in many cases POs will need a new structure to manage the processing business effectively. It may be necessary to create a separate, PO-owned company to manage the processing unit and, in addition, to create a second- or third-level organisation to manage the company and increase the scale of the business.
- *External barriers:* as we noted in Chapter 2, many processed goods face much higher import tariffs in industrialised countries, making it difficult for POs to compete in export markets in the North.

Processing is therefore not a straightforward activity and the decision to enter processing activities should be based on a thorough assessment of the market, the viability of the business model, and the capacity of the PO. For all but the simplest processing activities, this analysis should be conducted by professionals who have an in-depth understanding of the target market and the processing business. In Mozambique, for example, an Oxfam GB project providing simple oil-pressing equipment to producers failed because it was not based on a careful assessment of the market and the economic viability of processing oilseed.

FAs can play a useful role by helping POs access the necessary expertise to assess whether the proposed initiative is viable and to help the PO plan and implement the necessary investments. FAs can also support POs by helping them to develop the capacity of their leaders and managers and to access the necessary financing. However, as we noted above, financing investment through grants has disadvantages that FAs need to weigh up carefully.

Creating a brand

By creating a brand for one or more of the PO's products or creating a recognisable identity for the whole business, POs may be able to increase the perceived value of their products, in the eyes of buyers, and thereby charge higher prices. With the necessary packaging and branding, POs may also be able to access supermarkets and other retail markets and receive a much higher share of the retail price for their products. NASFAM, for example, sells packaged rice with the NASFAM logo in supermarkets in Malawi. In most cases, the main benefit of a brand for POs is to build buyers' confidence in the PO and the quality of their product. However, creating and maintaining a brand is a challenging and risky strategy for POs. It involves considerable investments and risks including:

- *Investing in product quality:* branding only works if POs can consistently produce products of the same quality and can consistently satisfy the demands of buyers or consumers, in terms of reliability, quantity, or quality. It may take a number of years for a PO to achieve this consistency and reliability but only one bad delivery to damage the PO's reputation and its brand. POs therefore need to make significant investments in production capacity, quality management and, where necessary, in appropriate packaging to preserve the quality of the product.
- *Investing in a brand and in brand promotion:* POs need to create a recognisable brand, in the form of an appropriate brand name or logo. If they are selling directly into retail markets, POs will also need to invest in appropriate labelling on their products as a means of promoting their brand. Zadrima, for example, invested in proper wine bottles and an attractive label in order to promote its product at a national trade fair. POs may be able to use creative and low-cost methods to advertise their product in domestic markets, but most do not have the resources to advertise their products in domestic markets, let alone export markets, unless they work in a partnership with an existing company. Kuapa Kokoo, for example, owns a share in

the Day Chocolate Company in the UK, which produces and markets a brand of chocolate (Divine Chocolate) for markets in Europe and the USA. Very few POs have the resources to create and maintain a brand, although all POs can gain significantly from developing and maintaining a good reputation for quality and reliability with buyers, whether or not they invest in creating a brand. FAs can provide support by helping POs access the necessary expertise to assess the costs and benefits of creating a brand and to support them through the process. FAs can also support investments in brand design, production capacity, and quality management to create the basic conditions for POs to develop a good reputation as the basis for building a brand in the future.

Advocacy

Small-scale producers tend to lack the capacity to influence the market environment and their interests are therefore frequently sidelined in the investment priorities of governments and large companies. Advocacy can enable small-scale producers to defend their rights and promote their interests in the market environment. However, although advocacy is important and can affect POs' survival, we are treating advocacy as an advanced activity because POs need considerable capacity and resources to undertake advocacy work, beyond simple, local advocacy initiatives. Some of the main challenges POs face in implementing effective advocacy work are:

- *Scale:* influence depends, at least in part, on the size of the organisation and the number of small-scale producers that are represented. This may require POs to expand, although growth driven by advocacy priorities may not be good for the business. A better strategy to increase scale is to join forces with other POs and organisations as part of a coalition, network, or a formal representative organisation. AProCA in West Africa, for example, operates as a representative lobbying organisation on behalf of its national PO member organisations.

- *Resources:* POs need skilled staff, additional office resources, and access to information networks to carry out research, develop policy positions, and lobby on behalf of their members at a local, national, or even international level. In practice, even large POs struggle to fund advocacy work from their own business profits and instead rely on grants to fund these activities. Individual members, especially women, often do not have the time to attend meetings and participate in lobbying activities and may need external financial support if they are to participate in such initiatives. OCDIH (Organismo Cristiano de Desarrollo Integral de Honduras), an FA in Honduras, has promoted

a system where group members undertake farm work for other members who spend time lobbying local politicians or attending meetings on behalf of the group.
- *Ownership and accountability:* if a PO generates sufficient business profits to fund advocacy work, it can only use this surplus if members are willing to forego higher payments in order to support the PO's lobbying activity. This requires that grassroots members understand the need for advocacy, and value this service. In large POs, where there is considerable distance between grassroots members and the board of directors, there is a danger that the directors may pay more attention to the advocacy priorities of FAs and other donors, especially if these external donors fund the PO's advocacy work. For example, when AProCA was first set up (see Chapter 10), some member POs felt that the new association was being driven by external priorities rather than those of individual members, which led to tensions within the new structure.
- *Internal tension:* if an FA decides to fund a PO's advocacy work this can create a mixed message: on the one hand, the FA emphasises financial sustainability in all its dealings with the PO, whilst on the other hand, the FA is willing to provide grants to the PO for a specific activity that the FA thinks is important. These different approaches can also confuse priorities within the PO or divert resources away from managing the business. Some POs therefore leave advocacy work to other organisations or create separate structures that are either owned by or affiliated to the PO to carry out policy and advocacy activities.
- *Increased profile:* advocacy work increases the profile of POs and therefore invites public attention and accountability. POs and FAs need to understand these risks and prepare for them before they engage in high-profile advocacy work, especially on sensitive issues.

Despite these challenges, many POs have no choice but to engage in advocacy activities to protect their members' livelihoods. As we saw in Case Study 8, Asprepatía emerged out of a campaign by producers to prevent the construction of a large sugar mill, which would have threatened their livelihood. Table 15.1 identifies four different roles FAs can play to facilitate POs' advocacy work.

Table 15.1: FA advocacy roles

FA role	Explanation
Lobbying for and with POs	Until POs have reached the scale and developed the capacity necessary to defend and promote their own interests, FAs may need to lobby with or on behalf of POs when they face serious challenges in the market environment. The Clam Clubs in Viet Nam, for example, do not have the capacity to lobby for a change in the laws governing POs, and rely on Oxfam GB and other organisations to lobby on their behalf.
Advocacy funding	As few POs generate sufficient income to fund their own advocacy work, FAs may need to fund such activities. However, FAs need to be aware of the challenges outlined above and help POs develop the necessary structure and internal accountability to ensure these activities are managed effectively and do not weaken the PO's business.
Capacity development	FAs often have considerable advocacy skills and experience within their organisation and can play an important role developing the policy and advocacy skills of POs.
Networking	Many FAs have strong links to national and international policy and advocacy networks and can help POs link into these. FAs may also help POs to set up new advocacy networks within their own country. Oxfam GB, for example, has supported MAPRONET, a network of POs providing business and advocacy services to its member POs in Ghana.

As POs often have to respond to threats in the market environment long before their business generates the resources required to fund lobbying activities, FAs can sometimes play an important bridging role by lobbying on behalf of POs. However, if advocacy is a high priority for a PO then the FA needs to focus on developing the PO's capacity to lobby on behalf of its members through appropriate funding arrangements, direct capacity development, and by linking POs into networks.

Summary: supporting advanced PO activities

- Processing can offer real benefits to producers if it is based on a sound business strategy, but POs have to overcome significant challenges and develop considerable skills to manage processing activities profitably.
- Creating a brand can enable POs to access higher prices, but building a brand is a costly and high-risk business strategy that requires large investments in quality, reputation, and brand recognition that few POs can afford.
- Advocacy is an important strategy that enables POs to defend their rights and promote their interests in the market environment. Effective advocacy requires skills, resources, and contacts that few POs can finance from their business profits. FAs can provide funding, training, and access to networks.

16 | Forming new producer organisations

As highlighted in Case Study 9 (see Chapter 13), forming new POs is a difficult task. To be sustainable, POs need to be built on a strong foundation of producer initiative and ownership. When an FA initiates the formation of a new PO it is difficult for the FA to judge whether this strong foundation is present, and the FA's involvement in the process can weaken the foundation. Forming new POs should therefore generally be approached as a last resort, and wherever possible FAs should try to work with existing POs rather than creating new organisations. The following points provide a brief summary of the main steps and issues FAs need to consider when facilitating the formation of new POs from individual producers or out of existing rural organisations, such as community-based organisations or self-help groups. Annex 1 lists various materials that provide more detailed guidance.

- *Raising awareness:* ideally, producers will already have expressed an interest in forming a PO and may even have taken the first step to bring a group of interested producers together. In this case, the FA can help explain how POs work and what steps are required to set up a collective marketing initiative. However, if FAs are starting from scratch and producers have not yet had the idea to work together, the task is more difficult. The challenge is to facilitate a process that results in the participants taking the main initiative to work together. Members' willingness to contribute their own resources to start the first collective activities provides a good test of their ownership of the new PO. Annex 5 provides some useful questions to help FAs assess whether a new initiative is based on a strong foundation.
- *Identifying participants:* as ownership and social capital are important for the success of the PO, FAs should avoid getting closely involved in the selection of members or imposing their own criteria on who can

or cannot participate. The more freedom producers have in deciding whom to work with, the more likely it is that the group will work well together. However, without any conditions or criteria on membership, new groups can be driven by the interests of powerful individuals within the community, which may lead to the exclusion of women or marginalised members of the community. In some cases, FAs may be able to persuade new groups to include women and other excluded community members without undermining trust and commitment within the group. Where this is not possible, FAs will need to consider alternative strategies, such as helping women establish their own separate groups, or additional support activities to increase the capacity of women and poorer members to participate effectively in the new PO (see section 14.1 for other strategies).

- *Group size:* group size should be kept small, ideally between 15 and 30 members, to facilitate good communication and regular interactions between all group members.
- *First meetings:* a new group needs to follow a simplified business-planning process, starting with an assessment of market opportunities before defining the group's objective and developing a very simple marketing strategy. It is also important at this stage to define how the group will divide any proceeds from their collective activities.
- *Pilot activities:* before the FA or individual members invest significant resources in the group, it is a good idea for the group to gain experience and test its marketing strategy through various pilot activities. New POs should focus on very simple collective activities and services for members, based on participants' existing livelihood activities. At this stage, FAs need to find the right balance between allowing the new PO to learn from its own experience and failures, and using its influence to help members avoid bad decisions that may undermine their confidence.
- *Consolidation:* if the pilot activities are successful, the group can begin to invest and expand its activities and gradually develop a simple decision-making structure. From the very start FAs need to help POs to develop a market-oriented approach and to focus on financially sustainable PO services and activities.
- *Financing:* most new POs will depend on the FA for access to start-up funding. Generally, it is better for FAs to provide access to loans rather than offering grants, as grants can exaggerate the profitability of the PO and undermine the members' sense of responsibility. If the FA does decide to offer a grant for operational funds or specific investments, the timing is critical: if a grant is offered too soon, before

the group has established itself, it can undermine the initiative and sense of ownership within the group.

- *Shared assets:* managing shared assets requires considerable social capital and management skills, and FAs should therefore avoid financing shared assets, such as tractors or processing equipment, until groups have gained experience and developed their capacity. Women's POs may however be an exception to this rule, as research suggests that women's groups are sometimes more successful at managing shared assets from an early stage.[46]
- *Transforming community-based groups into POs:* existing community-based groups may already have significant social capital. The challenge is to ensure that the members of such groups understand that the new group will function as an independent business and that they are prepared to take ownership of the business, including the risks involved.

Where possible FAs should involve other organisations, in particular local organisations, in the formation process. Not only do local organisations have a better understanding of the local context and local producers, but if other supporting organisations are involved from the start, they are likely to have a greater commitment to supporting the PO, which can reduce the new PO's dependency on a single FA.

Summary: forming new POs

- POs that are formed, primarily, in response to external initiative will often struggle to develop into sustainable businesses and organisations, and FAs should therefore avoid forming new POs, except as a last resort.
- Where FAs decide to form new POs, their aim should be to facilitate a process that results in producers taking the initiative to set up the PO and in the new members driving the process, rather than the FA driving it.

Endnotes

1. See for example Prinz 2002; van Dooren 1982.
2. See for example DFID 2005; IFAD 2001; World Bank 2005.
3. Dorward *et al.* 2004a.
4. This section is based on findings in: Dorward *et al.* 2004a and 2004b; IFAD 2001; Leys 1996; Todaro 2000; World Bank 1994.
5. Todaro 1992, p. 251.
6. See for example the 1981 Berg Report, World Bank 1981.
7. IFAD 2001.
8. World Bank 1994.
9. Kydd and Dorward 2004.
10. Dorward *et al.* 2004b; Jayne *et al.* 2005.
11. Kydd and Dorward 2004.
12. This section draws on: Aksoy and Beghin 2005; FAO 2005; Majluf 2004; Oxfam 2002; Suppan 2001; Watkins and von Braun 2003.
13. Oxfam 2002, p.124.
14. *Ibid.* p.113.
15. *Ibid.* p.117.
16. *Ibid.* p.106; Aksoy and Beghin 2005.
17. Watkins and von Braun 2003, p.13.
18. This distinction is based on Reardon and Timmer 2005.
19. Diao *et al.* 2003, p. vi.
20. This section draws on: Humphrey 2005; Lundy *et al.* 2004; Oxfam 2002.
21. Lundy *et al.* 2005a, p. 6.
22. This section draws on: Boselie and van de Kop 2005; Humphrey 2005; Lundy *et al.* 2004 and 2005a; Reardon *et al.* 2001; Ritson 1997; Vorley and Fox 2004.

23 Humphrey 2005, p. 8.
24 This section draws on: Boselie and van de Kop 2005; DFID 2004; Humphrey 2005; Ponte 2001; Vorley 2001; Vorley and Fox 2004.
25 Ponte 2001, p.18.
26 See Dorward *et al.* 1998 for further discussion.
27 This section is based on Humphrey 2005 and Lundy *et al.* 2004.
28 This section draws on: Balsevich *et al.* 2003; Humphrey 2005; Reardon *et al.* 2001 and 2003; Vorley 2001; Vorley and Fox 2004; Weatherspoon and Reardon 2003.
29 IFAD 2001, p. 184.
30 Reardon *et al.* 2003, p. 1142.
31 Reardon *et al.* 2003.
32 This section draws on: Balsevich *et al.* 2003; Giovannucci and Reardon (no date), Reardon *et al.* 2001.
33 This section draws on: Boselie and van de Kop 2005; Coulter *et al.* 1999; Dorward *et al.* 1998; Vorley and Fox 2004.
34 Cook and Iliopoulos 1999.
35 This estimate is based on findings in Devereux 2000; Jayne *et al.* 2005; and Rosegrant *et al.* 2006.
36 See for example Chirwa *et al.* 2005; Koopmans 2004; Stringfellow *et al.* 1997.
37 The names of some of these POs have been changed.
38 For more details see: Cook and Iliopoulos 1999; Hendrikse and Veerman 2001; Knight *et al.* 2003; Roth and Lyne 2003.
39 The guidance and good practice outlined in Part III draw on the case studies and examples cited throughout this guide, a workshop conducted in February 2006 with Oxfam staff working with POs, the author's own experience, and the following materials: Batt 2004; Bingen *et al.* 2003; Braverman *et al.* 1991; Chirwa *et al.* 2005; CLUSA no date; Coulter *et al.* 1999; Ellman *et al.* 2004; Harper 1992; Harper and Roy 2000; Hellin and Higman 2002; Hughes 1994; Koopmans 2004; Oxfam 2005; Robbins *et al.* 2004; Stringfellow *et al.* 1997.
40 This model is adapted from an exit strategy presented in Lundy *et al.* 2005b, p.24.
41 See Bingen *et al.* 2003 for more details.
42 The use of the term 'market literacy' is adapted here from Albu and Griffith 2005, p. 8.
43 See for example Harper and Roy 2000; Stringfellow *et al.* 1997.
44 Lundy *et al.* 2004, p.42.
45 This list is based on Hughes 1994.
46 See for example Stringfellow *et al.* 1997.

Annex 1 | Further reading and resources

This is a list of useful resources for background reading. For full references for each of these resources please consult the bibliography on p.170.

Chapter 2: Small-scale producers and the market
'False promise or false premise? The experience of food and input market reform in Eastern and Southern Africa', Jayne et al. (2001)
'The State of Food and Agriculture', FAO (2005)
'Rigged Rules and Double Standards: Trade Globalisation and the Fight against Poverty', Oxfam (2002)
Shaping Value Chains for Development: Global Value Chains for Agribusiness, Humphrey (2005)
'The rise of supermarkets in Africa, Asia and Latin America', Reardon et al. (2003)

Chapter 13: Initial steps and considerations
See Annex 2 for a tool on rapid assessment of markets and producers.
Mapping the Market: A Framework for Rural Enterprise Development Policy and Practice, Albu and Griffith (2005)
A Guide to Developing Partnerships, Territorial Analysis and Planning Together, Manual 1: Territorial Approach to Rural Agro-enterprise Development, Lundy et al. (2005b)
Identifying and Assessing Market Opportunities for Small-Scale Rural Producers, Manual 2: Territorial Approach to Rural Agro-enterprise, Ostertag (2004)

Chapter 14: Facilitating the producer organisation support process

Empowering grassroots members

'Linking farmers to markets: different approaches to human capital development', Bingen *et al.* (2003)
'Skills and Literacy Training for Better Livelihoods: A Review of Approaches and Experience', Oxenham *et al.* (2004)
Enhancing Farmers' Financial Management Skills, Heney (2000)
The Oxfam Gender Training Manual, Williams *et al.* (1995)
Leadership Training Manuel for Women Leaders of Co-operatives, ILO (2005)

Strengthening governance and leadership

Action Learning, A Practical Guide, Weinstein (2002)

Supporting market research

See Annex 2 for a tool on rapid assessment of markets and producers.
Marketing for Small-Scale Producers, Ad de veld (2004)
Clients First! A Rapid Market Appraisal (RMA) Tool Kit, Helvetas (2004)
Identifying and Assessing Market Opportunities for Small-Scale Rural Producers, Ostertag (2004)
Finding the Money: Farmer Organisation's Guide to Marketing for Small-Scale Farmers in Southern Africa, Lutz (2006)
'Agroindustrial investment and operations: identifying, developing and servicing markets and marketing strategies', Hughes (1994)

Facilitating effective business management

See Annex 3 for a tool on PO capacity appraisal and Annex 4 for a tool to help assess the potential implications of different legal structures.
Farmer-Controlled Economic Initiatives: Starting a Cooperative, Koopmans (2004)
Into the Market Manual, Traidcraft (2004)
Strategic Planning Handbook for Cooperatives, Namken and Rapp (1997)

Improving the product

Helping Small Farmers Think About Better Growing and Marketing: A Reference Manual, FAO (2004)
'Understanding Grades and Standards and How to Apply Them', Giovannucci and Reardon (no date)
Into the Market Manual, Traidcraft (2004)
'Small producers in export horticulture – a guide to best practice', NRI (2003)
Fairtrade Labelling Organisation: www.fairtrade.net/ and http://www.flo-cert.net/
EurepGAP: www.eurepgap.org/Languages/English/index_html

Supporting appropriate producer organisation structures

See Annex 4 for a tool to help assess the potential implications of different legal structures.

'Co-ops 101: An Introduction to Cooperatives', Frederick (1997)

Facilitating trade linkages

Increasing the Competitiveness of Market Chains for Smallholder Producers, Lundy et al. (2004)

Building Agri-Supply Chains: Issues and Guidelines, van Roekel et al. (2002)

Making the Most of Trade Fair Participation – a Toolkit, Traidcraft (no date)

'Linking farmers to markets: a manual for helping smallholder farmers access markets by working with commercial companies' (Oxfam GB internal document), Ellman et al. (2004)

Chain Empowerment: Supporting African Farmers to Develop Markets, KIT, Faida MaLi and IIRR (2006)

Facilitating access to business services

Mapping the Market: A Framework for Rural Enterprise Development Policy and Practice, Albu and Griffith (2005)

Chapter 15: Supporting advanced producer organisation activities

Processing

Strategies for Diversification and Adding Value to Food Exports: A Value Chain Perspective, Humphrey and Oetero (2000)

Advocacy

Power Tools: Handbook to Tools and Resources for Policy Influence in Natural Resource Management, Vermeulen (2005)

Chapter 16: Forming new producer organisations

Farmer-Controlled Economic Initiatives: Starting a Cooperative, Koopmans (2004)

Advice Manual for the Organisation of Collective Marketing Activities for Small-scale Farmers, Robbins et al. (2004)

'Considering cooperation: a guide for new cooperative development', Henehan and Anderson (2001)

Basic Accounting for Small Groups, Cammack (2002)

Building Capacity Through Financial Management: A Practical Guide, Cammack (2007)

Annex 2 | Rapid assessment of markets and producers

This tool is designed to support the facilitating agency (FA) in undertaking two different types of activities:
- Contract an internal or external market specialist to conduct a market and producer assessment as a basis for assessing viability and for planning PO support activities. This assessment should identify whether there are potential sustainable economic activities for small-scale producers in the target area, and what these are. The questions listed in the tool should enable FA staff to manage the assessment and appraise the results of this work. Where possible this analysis should involve or be undertaken by target producers, facilitated by the market specialist. Where possible, other local market actors should be involved or interviewed.
- Facilitate initial market research managed or undertaken by a PO. The tool can be used by FA staff as a checklist to help POs consider key questions and issues in their initial market research and in their assessment of possible market options.

1. Assessment process

- Will the process consider and consult with a broad enough range of stakeholders?
- How will the targeted male and female producers participate in market selection?

2. Small-scale producers, opportunities, and challenges

Which are the best production and processing opportunities for male and female small-scale producers?

Current and potential activities

- What different types of male and female small-scale producers operate in the target area by production, socio-economic, market engagement, and organisation levels?
- What production and marketing activities are men and women involved in, in the local area, and where are their products traded?
- Is there sufficient demand in the existing markets producers are engaged in to absorb the production of additional producers without significantly affecting prices?
- What different types of production are different categories of producer (e.g. 'elite', large-scale, subsistence, men and women) involved in within the region?
- If a potential new crop or production method has been identified, will male and female producers invest in this? What proportion of producers' income/time will be generated/required by this product/market?
- What proportion of income generated will benefit women directly or indirectly?
- What are the main issues and constraints facing local enterprises in terms of:
    - participating households' ability to invest in the market, incorporating social (include time constraints), political, and economic limitations?
    - challenges in the market chain?
    - challenges in the market environment?
    - access to affordable market services?*
- What are the constraints, problems, and opportunities specific to women producers?
- How vulnerable are participating households to shocks, trends, and seasonality insofar as this may affect production/marketing?

Collective capacity

- What existing POs/enterprises are there in the local area and are they involved in the potential markets identified? If not, which markets are they involved in? Are they business-oriented? How effective are they at what they do?
- What proportion of the POs' membership consists of women? Are women in leadership roles in these POs? What opportunities are there for women to enter these POs and gain leadership?

- What previous experience is there of collective action (around any issue) within the community? Are there any groups of people likely to be excluded from collective marketing activities? Do women need separate POs?
- What incentives/disincentives are there to join/not join POs? Is collective production and/or marketing an effective strategy?

Other organisations and institutions working in the markets or region

- Are there business-oriented partners that the FA and/or PO can potentially work with, with experience of the differing needs of men and women? What level of capacity do they have?
- What government agencies, NGOs, specialist support agencies (local, national, and international) and private companies are active in the local area/markets and active in enterprise development? What assistance or challenges do they provide for small-scale producers and POs?
- What services do government departments/agencies provide to small businesses, including POs, in the region?
- How strong are these POs in terms of their business capacity, governance and management capacity, and the empowerment of grassroots members?

3. Regional overview

- What value chain or market analysis already exists?
- What are the key commodities, processed products, or semi-finished goods demanded by major retailers or processing companies in surrounding districts?
- What are the main products traded in local markets and where do they come from?
- What activities could men and women be involved in?
- What are the new activities that women could be involved in as producers, as traders, or as value-adders/processors?
- What local products are currently being traded in regional, national, or even international markets, and which ones have a competitive advantage** in these markets?
- What are the main problems and constraints facing local enterprises in terms of:
  - the functioning of the market chain?
  - the market environment?

- access to affordable market services?
- Are there local market services? Who provides these (dedicated specialist support agencies, POs, other businesses, government agencies, NGOs, etc.)?
- What are the main problems and constraints faced by traders?
- What are the additional/specific constraints faced by women small-scale producers?
- How vulnerable is the market to shocks, trends, and seasonality?
- How vulnerable are participating households to shocks, trends, and seasonality, insofar as this will affect production/marketing?

4. National overview

Comparing results from the national level with those from the local level, which markets have the greatest potential for project involvement for target beneficiaries? This analysis should include:

- Major markets by numbers of men and women engaged
- Involvement of poor men, poor women (by market)
- Role of women, type of work done (e.g. wage work/management / ownership) by market
- Markets which FA or FA partners have previous experience in
- Overview of major trends in market constraints/opportunities
- Existence of unacceptable working conditions for male and female workers
- Seasonality of demand by product, seasonality of supply by product
- Which of these products/enterprises the target community or region can produce or get involved in

* Market services include production, finance, transportation, and business-development services.
** Competitive advantage exists when consumers can be offered greater value, either through sustainable lower prices or by providing greater benefits and services that justify higher prices.

Annex 3 | Producer organisation capacity appraisal

This aim of this tool is to help facilitating agencies (FAs) and POs to assess the capacity-development needs and priorities of POs.

Assessing a PO's capacity is not a matter of ticking boxes. While a simple checklist can help, there are some areas of capacity such as grassroots ownership or business strategy, that cannot be assessed meaningfully by ticking boxes or using a scoring system. There is also a risk that FAs will use such checklists to conduct *their* assessment of the PO, which may feel threatening to PO members and undermine their trust and openness. This trust and openness is essential because effective capacity development depends on the PO recognising where it needs to develop its capacity – it is not enough for the FA to recognise the PO's weaknesses. We suggest that this appraisal tool is used in one of the following two ways:

1. As a guide/checklist to help FAs assess a PO's capacity *with* PO staff and to structure discussions with POs on development needs and priorities.

2. As a guide for POs to assess their own capacity.

The appraisal tool is divided into nine sections. Each section starts with a summary of the core capacities that POs generally need to develop to become strong and sustainable businesses and organisations. Not all of these core capacities will be relevant, so the tool should be adapted according to the context. POs may find it useful to assess their own capacity against each of these core capacities, using a scale of 1 to 5 where 1 is low and 5 is high. These core capacities are followed by a set of questions to support further analysis.

1. Capacity of grassroots members

Core capacities   **Score 1–5**

- PO members/staff have basic understanding of the PO and feel responsible for its success
- Women and other marginalised groups are able to participate in decision-making of the PO on an equal basis and are not constrained by limited confidence, time, capacity, or other members' attitudes
- PO members have the necessary knowledge, skills, and confidence to participate in decision-making
- PO members see themselves as the owners of the organisation and feel responsible for its success

Further analysis

- Do women and men have the same opportunities in the PO (skill development, promotion, participation in decision-making, etc.)?
- Are the PO's vision and mission known and understood by most people in the PO?
- Do members have the literacy, numeracy, and skills to understand the PO's constitution, financial reports, and business plans?
- Do PO staff have the necessary skills to carry out their duties or, if not, are adequate training plans in place?
- Do members have the confidence to participate actively in management and organisational meetings and at the PO's annual general meeting?
- Are all categories of members (e.g. men and women, members of different social or ethnic groups) represented in the PO's leadership, at each level of the PO?
- Do members make any voluntary contributions to their PO that may indicate a sense of ownership?
- How easy is it for members, in particular women or members of other marginalised groups, to stand for election and become leaders?

2. Organisational governance and management

Core capacities   **Score 1–5**

- PO's constitution or other written documents clearly define its purpose, governance rules, structure, and duties/responsibility of members, leaders, and managers
- PO leaders have limited terms in office and stand down when their term is completed
- PO leaders understand the business and are able to manage any hired business managers
- Members/staff have trust and confidence in the leadership and managers
- Leaders are able to respond to and manage internal and external change

Further analysis
Governance rules and structure
- Does the PO have a clear and non-discriminatory membership policy?
- Do the PO's leaders and members/staff have a clear understanding of their individual roles, functions, and responsibilities within the PO?
  - Does the PO have a written constitution or charter (e.g. statutes or internal rules including defined roles for staff or committee members)?
  - Is there an up-to-date organigram (i.e. a diagram showing how the PO is organised)?
- How effective is the PO's governance structure in ensuring managers are accountable to members but also have sufficient freedom to run the business effectively?
- Are the PO's governance structures fair and transparent and do they clearly define the authority and responsibilities of members, leaders, and managers?
- Do plans exist to increase the capacity of marginalised members to participate in the PO's decision-making processes?
- Are there mechanisms in place (group meetings, trade union representation etc.) for consulting members and employees on business decisions?

Social capital
- Do PO members see the PO as their own idea and their own organisation? Do they talk about the PO as an external initiative?
- Are members committed to the PO and willing to forego short-term benefits to secure long-term gains?
- To what extent do members trust the leaders/managers of the PO?
- Is communication effective within individual groups and between different levels of the PO?

Leadership
- Do the PO's leaders have a clear vision for the PO?
- Do the PO's leaders and managers have the necessary leadership and management skills to perform their tasks effectively or are plans in place to train them?
- Does the PO have rules that prevent conflicts of interest between leaders' political engagements and representing members' interests?
- Are the PO's leaders aware of the organisation's culture and how this affects behaviour and attitudes within the PO?

3. PO structure   Score 1–5

Core capacities
- PO's legal structure fits its business needs and organisational priorities
- PO's size, structure, and growth plans are based on business needs defined in a business strategy
- PO's growth plans are sustainable and realistic in terms of existing level of business income, management capacity, and social capital

Further analysis
- Who owns the PO and how are benefits distributed from PO activities?
- Is the PO's legal structure the best fit within the existing legal framework of the country?
- Is the PO legally registered? Are taxes paid to the government? Does the PO have title to land/property?
- How well does the organisational structure fit the business needs and the demands of the markets the PO is operating in?
- Does the PO have a realistic growth strategy based on a business and market strategy?
- Do accountability and communication systems within the PO need to change to reflect any planned expansion in the future?

4. Marketing capacity   Score 1–5

Core capacities
- PO applies a market-oriented approach to all its activities and services
- PO has the capacity to conduct or manage market research and evaluate market opportunities
- PO has a marketing strategy based on a market assessment, the priorities of members, and the PO's production and marketing capacity
- PO's marketing strategy takes into account potential market risks to its members

Further analysis
Market research capacity
- Does the PO have the resources to manage market research independently?
  - Have staff undertaken shop and market visits?
  - Does the PO know who its competitors are in the target market(s)?
- Can the PO assess different market opportunities and select options?
  - What were the PO's approximate sales and costs (by percentage or in hard currency value) in the last financial year and the number of buyers for each market, e.g. local markets/traders, export markets, processors?
- Does the PO have access to up-to-date market information?
  - From where is market information on market demand, future trends, competition, etc. obtained?

Marketing strategy
- Does the PO's marketing strategy reflect its competitive advantage and the capacity of PO members and managers?
  - Is there someone in charge of marketing and sales?
  - Can the PO communicate in the language of target markets?
- Does the PO have a strategy for increasing the number of customers?

- How does the PO promote its business and communicate with customers and suppliers, e.g. irregular meetings, planned meetings, letters, email, telephone, fax, catalogues, leaflets, website?
- Does the PO have the capacity to implement the marketing strategy successfully, i.e. do members have sufficient production capacity and do managers have adequate marketing skills?
- Does the PO have an export licence?
- To what extent does the PO's marketing strategy balance profitability and risk?

5. Business management   Score 1–5

Core capacities
- PO has a clear and realistic business strategy set out in a business plan
- PO's business is able to cover its costs and pay suppliers/members or, if not, a realistic plan to cover these costs within a defined timeframe
- PO's business strategy clearly accounts for the cost of business services that are currently funded by donors
- PO has an efficient and transparent payment and cash-flow system that enables it to pay its members and service providers on a timely basis
- PO has access to sustainable financing sources

Further analysis
Business planning
- Does the PO have a business plan written by managers/leaders covering several years?
- Do PO leaders/managers have the capacity to develop business plans?
- Is the PO's strategy, outlined in the business plan, consistent with its current activities and finances?
- What investments, e.g. new equipment, will the PO require to achieve its business targets?
- Do the leaders/managers and members see the PO as an independent business that has to become financially sustainable?
- Do PO members value the services provided by the PO and is this reflected in stable membership numbers or rising membership over preceding years?

Financial management
- Are PO managers able to assess the profitability of the business based on an assessment of actual and hidden costs?
- Does the PO have access to long-term affordable financing to fund operational and investment plans?
    - Has the PO ever received a bank loan?
- Does the PO have an annual budget and does it produce regular financial reports?
- Is the PO's payment system to members/staff transparent and understood by all members?

- Are wages above the legal minimum? Are women paid the same as men for work of equal value?
- Does the PO have an effective cash-flow management system?
- Does the PO have an efficient and transparent system for distributing business profits to its members?

Financial systems
- Does the PO have trained accounting staff and effective accounting systems?
- Does an independent auditor audit the PO's accounts?
- Does the PO have the equipment and resources to manage its finances efficiently and securely?

Operational management
- Does the PO have adequate office facilities and communications infrastructure to conduct its business?
- Is the PO aware of any positive or negative impact it has on the natural environment?
- Do the managers have the necessary experience and skills to manage the business effectively?
  - Can the PO react to buyers' requests in a timely manner? Does the PO need to develop the capacity of its staff in key areas and does it have the resources to fund these investments?

6. Production capacity   Score 1–5

Core capacities
- Leaders/managers understand the quantity, quality, and reliability demands of buyers and can keep in touch with changing demands
- PO has logistical systems to co-ordinate members' production to meet market demand
- PO has quality management and internal incentive systems to meet market demands
- PO's investments in quality management, productivity, or certification will generate the income necessary to cover the ongoing costs of these investments

Further analysis
- Do managers understand buyers' preferences and the standards demanded by target markets?
  - Does the PO have specifications for its products?
  - Is the PO aware of legal regulations concerning its products, e.g. food-safety regulations?
  - Does the product require special packaging? If so, is this done by the PO?
- Does the PO need to upgrade producers' skills or make investment in technology?

- Do premises/workplace have sufficient space, illumination, and ventilation? Are there health risks?
- Does the PO have the systems and resources to gain independent certification of its products?
- Do producers have the capacity to produce the quality and quantity of products demanded by buyers?
  - Is there a production plan and is the PO's production capacity known?
  - Does the PO have sufficient equipment for production?
  - Where are the products stored?
- Does the PO have the necessary systems and resources to monitor and control production quality?
  - Does the PO have an inventory of stocks and/or equipment, managed by someone?
  - Have problems which could/do affect production been detected? (What are the major problems e.g. quality of raw materials, lack of credit or stocks etc.)?
- Do members understand, support, and trust the PO's quality management and related incentives system?
  - Are there records of rejected products, customer complaints, raw materials, productivity etc.?
  - What happens to rejected products? (Is there a system for rejecting sub-standard products and removing them from normal sales?)

7. Market linkages   Score 1–5

Core capacities
- PO has sufficient bargaining power to negotiate acceptable prices and good terms
- Managers/leaders have confidence to negotiate sales
- PO is able to assess market opportunities and up-to-date market information
- PO has a good reputation with buyers for quality and reliability

Further analysis
- Do PO staff have the experience, confidence, and skills to negotiate business deals independently?
  - What local, national, and international networks is the PO a member of?
- What competitive advantage does the PO have in each marketing chain it operates in, e.g. price, quality, scarcity of its product, its size, traditional design etc.?
- Can the PO identify new market opportunities and select options?
- How often does it meet or discuss business with current buyers?
- Does the PO keep a record of buyers and potential buyers?
- Does the PO have confidence that member producers or suppliers will honour advance contracts, even if they are offered better prices by other buyers?

- Does the PO have experience of working with target traders, e.g. local traders, processors, wholesalers, direct consumers, export agents?
- Is the PO's reputation in the market based on its business record or the involvement of another party, e.g. a specialist support agency?

8. Access to business services   Score 1–5

Core capacities
- PO is able to access all necessary business and development support services
- PO has a long-term strategy to finance business services from business revenue
- Leaders/managers have the capacity to negotiate service contracts

Further analysis
- Do leaders/managers have the capacity to assess what business service the PO needs e.g. transport, insurance, production training?
- Can the PO access and afford the business services it needs to conduct and develop its business?
- Does the PO have a strategy to access essential business services that are currently unavailable?
- Will the PO have the resources and capacity to access and afford independent business services once the FA withdraws its support?

9. Advocacy capacity   Score 1–5

Core capacities
- PO can defend and promote its own/its members' interests in the market environment
- PO has the necessary skills, financing, structure, and networks to conduct effective advocacy work (if it is a priority)
- PO's advocacy priorities are driven by the needs and priorities of its members

Further analysis
- Do leaders/managers have the time, confidence, and skills to negotiate or meet with other representative organisations and policy makers?
- Does the PO have access to the research and policy resources and networks necessary to conduct effective advocacy work?
- How are members/staff compensated for giving up time to lobby external organisations or attend meetings?
- If the PO plans to do or is already engaged in advocacy work, whose advocacy priorities and interests are driving this work?
- Does the PO have the financial resources to fund existing or planned advocacy activities and, if not, how will it fund these in the long run?
- What steps will the PO take to ensure that any existing or planned advocacy work does not divert essential resources away from the business?

Annex 4 | Potential implication of different legal structures

The following table provides an overview of some of the most important characteristics of the five legal structures introduced in Chapter 6. Each of these structures, if they exist within a country's legal framework, will be defined in slightly different ways and with different terminology from country to country. For this reason, the information in this table should only be used as an initial rough guide to help facilitating agencies (FAs) and POs consider potential implications of different options in relation to a PO's business and organisational needs. POs will need to consult legal experts and existing POs in their country to get a detailed picture of the options available to them. In some cases this consultation will highlight the need for changes to the current legal framework to create suitable options for POs. In this case FAs may need to invest resources to lobby for such changes before supporting PO development directly.

	Informal organisation	Association	Traditional co-operative	New generation co-operative	Private company
Main purpose	Competing in informal markets	Providing services to members	Providing services for members	Providing service and generating a profit for members	Generating a profit for shareholders on their investment
Owners	Participants	Members or board of directors	Members	Members or shareholders	Shareholders
Membership rules	Up to the members	Open membership; non-active members permitted (depends on rules of the association)	Open membership; only active members	Membership closed and based on fixed supply contracts	Could be limited to maximum number
Voting rights	Up to the members	Flexible: depends on rules of association; usually one vote per person	One member, one vote	Based on value of supply contracts	Based on number of shares
Decision-making structure	Up to the members	Flexible: depends on rules of association	Board of directors elected by members	Board of directors elected by members/shareholders	Board of directors elected by shareholders
Principle for distributing profits	Up to the members	Flexible or not permitted	Based on patronage	Based on shares/investment	Based on shares/investment
Risk to members (liability)	Participants personally liable for debts	Participants personally liable for debts	Members only liable for value of their investment	Members only liable for value of their investment	Shareholders only liable for value of their shares

Annex 4: Potential implication of different legal structures | 157

	Informal organisation	Association	Traditional co-operative	New generation co-operative	Private company
Regulation: external reporting requirements	None	Minimal	Financial statements, audit, and additional report	Financial statement and audit; may be additional report	Financial statements; audit depending on size of business
Costs of administration	Depends on complexity of activity	Depends on complexity of activity	Depends on complexity of activity but relatively high for simple collective activities	Depends on complexity of activity and size of business	Depends on complexity of activity and size of business
Access to financing from banks	None	Poor access as association has low business credibility	May have access to short-term loans but rarely to long-term financing	Probably better than traditional co-operatives	Usually better than co-operatives but depends on nature of business
Taxation	Individual members	Individual members	Individual members and, usually, no taxes or tax concessions on collective profits	Depends on structure; could be both company and individual shareholders	Both company and individual shareholders
Investment incentives	Depends on group rules	Depends on rules of association; if profits cannot be distributed incentives are low	Low as equal voting rights	High as voting rights proportional to investment	High as voting rights proportional to investment

	Informal organisation	Association	Traditional co-operative	New generation co-operative	Private company
Ability to transfer shares	n/a	n/a	Only to co-operative when members retire from membership	Possible with approval of other members	Depends on company's constitution but often flexible
Potential exposure to political interference	Low	Probably low but depends on local context	Can be high, depending on regulation. Particular risks in countries with history of state interference in co-operatives	Probably lower than traditional co-operatives but depends on local context	Probably lower than co-operatives but depends on local context

Annex 5 | Building blocks for a strong foundation

The following questions aim to help facilitating agencies (FAs) involved in forming new POs to assess whether a number of important building blocks that contribute to a strong PO foundation are present among the participants or potential members.

Building blocks	Critical questions
Basic motivation	• Is the participants' main motivation for forming or joining the group the desire to solve their own marketing problems or to access external assistance? • Do producers view group formation as a condition for accessing external assistance or resources? • Can the producers provide a clear explanation of why collective action is necessary and how it will improve their market access? • Do the producers have a shared experience of exploitation in the market, which they want to overcome through collective action?
Sense of ownership	• Do the producers want external assistance to support their own efforts to address their problems or do they expect external help to solve their problems for them? • Do the producers talk about the proposed PO as their own idea and their own organisation, even if it was first suggested by the FA, or do they talk about it as the FA's initiative and organisation? • Are the producers interested in discussing how the PO should be organised, what activities they should undertake, and who should be members, or do such discussions have to be initiated by the FA? • Are the producers willing to invest their own limited resources, including time, assets, and financial contributions, to set up the PO, before any external resources are offered, or do they expect all start-up resources to be provided by the FA?

Building blocks	Critical questions
Initiative	• Have individual or groups of producers already tried to address marketing problems in various ways? • Have the producers already shown initiative and taken steps, even if unsuccessful, to solve their problems or are they passively waiting for the FA to start the process?
Business orientation	• Do the producers talk about the proposed initiative as a business or commercial activity rather than a means of accessing support more easily? • Do the producers recognise a difference between the proposed PO and other types of community-based organisations which have been set up in the past? • Do at least some of the producers have entrepreneurial skills and experience selling products and dealing with traders? • Do at least some of the producers have production skills and experience of sharing practices with others and accessing production services?
Social capital	• Do the producers already have experience of working together successfully in informal marketing initiatives or in other joint community activities? • Have the producers already shown a commitment to work together by forming an informal organisation? • Do the producers who are interested in forming a PO all know each other? • Are they from the same local area/neighbourhood?

Glossary

adding value — Adding value to a product means increasing its economic value by processing, marketing, or branding the product. For example, processing apples into apple juice increases their economic value, as does marketing apples as organic apples.

aflatoxin — Aflatoxins are a naturally occurring toxin produced by a fungus that can affect many different crops, especially under moisture stress.

bargaining power — Bargaining power is the ability of a buyer or a seller to influence the price or the terms of a business transaction. Bargaining power depends on different factors including scarcity, the information both parties have about the product and prices, and whether either party has alternative marketing options.

bottom line — The bottom line is the net income of a business after all costs and liabilities have been deducted.

break even — To break even means that the total income from your business exactly covers your total business costs. If your income rises any further and your costs remain the same, you will make a profit.

bulk, bulking — Bulking means combining small quantities of a product from many producers into a large quantity, usually for sale.

cash flow — The amount of cash a PO will receive and the amount it needs to spend over a certain period of time.

certification	Product certification is a process designed to ensure that a product meets established product standards. Certification is usually carried out by an independent agency that has been authorised to test and certify producers by the government or an association, or a private company that has established the standard.
collateral	Collateral is a type of guarantee provided by a borrower to a lender in the form of property or other asset. If the borrower is unable to repay the loan the lender can claim the property or asset to recover the value of the loan. The purpose of collateral is to reduce the risk to the lender.
commodities	Commodities are products that are treated as if they always have the same quality (i.e. as a homogenous product) and so buyers and consumers are only interested in the quantity bought or sold. In the past, most agricultural products were traded as commodities and some, such as wheat, are still sold as commodities today.
competitive advantage	A producer has a competitive advantage over other producers if he or she can sell a product at a sustainable price which is lower than that of other producers, or if he or she can offer a better product (or better benefits and services with the product) that justifies a higher price.
co-ordination	Co-ordination in a market is the process of facilitating business transactions between buyers and sellers. In a developed market, this process usually occurs automatically as there are established mechanisms for finding buyers or sellers and reducing transaction costs. But in poor rural markets high transaction costs may lead to co-ordination failures, in which case external intervention by the government or other agencies may be necessary to facilitate transactions between buyers and sellers.
developed country	In this guide we use the term 'developed country' to refer to the 'over-developed', industrialised countries of the world, e.g. North America, Europe, Australia, etc.
developing country	In this guide we use the term 'developing country' to refer to the economically under-developed countries of the world which have a low to moderate Human Development Index, according to the UN Development Programme.

differentiation	Product differentiation means changing a product to make it different from the products sold by competitors and more attractive in the target market.
diversification	Producers can either diversify their products or their markets or a combination of both. Product diversification means producing a range of different products, while market diversification is producing the same product for different markets. Diversification is used to reduce risks and/or to increase profits by producing a higher value product or accessing a more profitable market.
domestic food markets	A domestic food market is the market for food products in a producer's own country.
economic actors	Economic actors are the buyers and sellers of goods or services who are active in the market.
economies of scale	Economies of scale are reductions in costs for each unit produced or marketed that result from increasing the scale of an activity.
embedded services	An embedded market service is a service that is provided as part of a business transaction. For example, an exporter may provide input services to farmers as part of a contract to buy the farmers' crop.
empowerment	Empowerment means increasing the confidence and capacity of an individual or group of people to influence their circumstances or take control of their situation by increasing their political, social, or economic strength.
extension services	Extension services are training and advisory services provided to farmers for crop cultivation or animal husbandry.
facilitating agency (FA)	FA is a term we introduce in Chapter 12 to describe a development NGO in their role of facilitating support to POs.
financially sustainable	A financially sustainable PO is a PO that can cover all its costs from its business income and generate satisfactory benefits for its members without external subsidies, such as grants.
fixed costs	Fixed costs are business costs which do not change in proportion to the scale or level of activity of a business.

For example, most businesses have overhead costs, such as equipment or rent, that are the same however many products the business sells. In contrast, variable costs, such as input costs or fuel, increase in direct proportion to the amount produced or sold.

food safety	Food safety refers to the processes and mechanisms at all stages of food production, handling, processing, transporting, and storing, designed to protect the food supply from chemical, bacterial, or physical dangers to the consumer's health.
grades and standards	Grades and standards are the technical specifications, definitions, and systems for sorting products into different quality, size, or other classes, established by governments or private companies to make trade easier or to differentiate products.
high-value products	In the context of agricultural marketing, high-value products typically refer to horticultural products (fruit and vegetables), floriculture (e.g. the cut-flower industry), or meat products.
holding company	A holding company is a company whose purpose is to own some or all the shares of another company.
informal market	An informal market is a market that is not regulated or governed by formal institutions. Generally, business transactions in an informal market are not taxed and are not protected by the law.
inputs	The materials and resources needed to produce a product, e.g. seeds, fertiliser, irrigation, labour.
input credit	Credit provided in the form of an input. Often input credit is provided on the condition that the producer sells the product produced with the inputs to the lender, which enables the lender to recover the cost of the input and the interest on the credit.
International Commodity Agreements	In the 1970s and 1980s the global production of commodities, such as coffee, was controlled through International Commodity Agreements between producer and consumer countries. These Agreements stabilised commodity prices by setting production quotas, i.e. limits on production, for producing countries.

margin, profit margin	A PO's profit margin is the proportion of sales' income that the PO keeps as profits. It is usually expressed as a percentage and is calculated by dividing net income (i.e. profit) by revenues (i.e. sales income).
market chain linkages	Market chain linkages are the connections between each stage of the market chain and usually consist of business transactions between buyers and sellers.
market chain	A market chain is a chain of economic actors, including producers, processors, traders, and retailers, who each play a part in getting a product from the production stage to the consumer. See the explanation and diagram in Chapter 2 (p 7).
market concentration	Market concentration means that there are only a small number of companies operating at one particular stage within a market chain. As a result these companies usually have a degree of market power and can influence the prices or terms of transactions.
market liberalisation	Market liberalisation or economic liberalisation refers to a set of economic policies which were introduced from the early 1980s and replaced previous economic policies that emphasised the role of the state in managing the economy. In developing countries, market liberalisation tried to limit the role of the state to supplying public goods and providing a so-called enabling policy environment.
market power	Market power is the ability of a buyer or seller to influence or dictate the price of the product they are buying or selling. Market power usually occurs when a company controls a large share of the market.
market services	Market services are the services producers and other actors in the market chain need to conduct their business. They include production, finance, transport, and business-development services, provided by the public or private sector.
market structure	Market structure usually refers to how competitive a market is. If a market is dominated by a small number of buyers who can influence prices then the structure is uncompetitive. A competitive market structure occurs when there are many buyers and sellers and no one can dictate the price.

market system	A market system involves a market or value chain, the market services provided in the chain, and the market environment.
middle-income country	Middle-income countries or 'newly industrialised countries' are countries such as Brazil or the Philippines, which have undergone a rapid process of economic growth. A common characteristic of such countries is a very unequal distribution of the benefits of this growth.
niche market	A niche market is a small portion of the market, represented by a specific group of existing or potential customers. Most speciality products are sold in niche markets.
non-tariff barriers	Non-tariff barriers to trade are restrictions on imports that are not based on taxing the imports. The most common are minimum health and food-safety standards, import quotas, and seasonal import restrictions.
Northern subsidies	Northern subsidies are the grants paid by the governments of many developed countries (e.g. North America and Europe) to lower the price of products to producers or consumers in those countries. These subsidies give producers in these countries an unfair advantage in the global market and, in the past, have encouraged over-production, which lowers world market prices.
organic	An agricultural product that is labelled 'organic' has been produced and certified according to organic standards that prohibit the use of chemical fertilisers, pesticides, or other artificial additives.
patronage	Patronage means to use a service. In a co-operative, for example, profits are distributed according to each member's patronage, i.e. how much each member has used the services of the PO. This is usually calculated according to the value of products each member has either sold or bought through the co-operative.
perishable goods	Perishable goods are goods that deteriorate (lose their quality) quickly, even without use. Many agricultural products, such as vegetables or milk, deteriorate quickly if they are not stored or processed appropriately.

portal company	A portal company is a type of PO that provides services to both members and non-members; for example, a trading company owned by a PO that buys crops from members and non-members.
processing	Processing is the process of changing the form of a product, usually into a more valuable form, e.g. processing milk into cheese, or grapes into wine.
produce	Produce is a general term for farm-produced goods.
scarcity, scarcity value	Scarcity means that something is in short supply relative to the demand, which results in the product having a high value, or scarcity value.
second-level organisation	A second-level organisation is the second level within a multi-level PO.
side-selling	If a producer makes an agreement to sell his or her produce to one buyer but then breaks the agreement and sells it to another instead, the producer is side-selling. Side-selling among PO members can be very damaging for a PO's reputation and business.
social capital	The term social capital is used in many different ways. In this guide we use it to mean the mutual trust and commitment between the different members of a PO.
speciality products	Speciality products are products that have special characteristics based on their quality, their origin, or how the product is produced.
starting capital	Starting capital is the money a business needs to start its activities and begin trading.
subsistence	A subsistence livelihood is a livelihood that is based on meeting all household consumption needs from one's own production.
tariffs	A tariff is a type of tax that is charged on imports or exports.
'thin' markets	A 'thin' market is a market with a low volume of trade or a low number of transactions.
third-level organisation	A third-level organisation is the highest level within a multi-level PO. Another name for this organisation is an apex or third-tier organisation.

transaction	A business transaction is the exchange of a product or service between a buyer and seller.
transaction costs	Transaction costs are the costs of doing business, including the costs and risks involved in searching for buyers and sellers, the cost of assessing the quality and other characteristics of a product, and the costs of negotiating a contract and making sure it is honoured.
value chain	A value chain refers to a strategic network of independent businesses that work together to ensure that what is produced, the production process, and the quantity and timing meet the demands of retailers or processors.
vertical integration	Vertical integration is a type of ownership in which a company owns more than one stage of a market or value chain. For example, a PO can vertically integrate 'forward' into processing by establishing its own processing plant, or it can vertically integrate 'backward' into input supply by setting up its own input-supply business.
voting rights	Voting rights are the number of votes individual members have to cast in elections or votes in a PO's general meeting.
wholesale market	A wholesale market is a market where goods are mostly sold in large quantities to retailers, processors, or other commercial users rather than to consumers.

Bibliography

All web references last checked April 2007.

Ad de veld (2004) *Marketing for Small-Scale Producers*, Wageningen: Agromisa Foundation, www.ruralfinance.org/servlet/BinaryDownloaderServlet/24576_Marketing_for_Small_.pdf?filename=1130257058906_agromisa_marketing.pdf&refID=24576

Aksoy, M. A. and Beghin, J. C. (eds.) (2005) *Global Agricultural Trade and Developing Countries*, Washington DC: World Bank.

Albu, M. and Griffith, A. (2005) *Mapping the Market: A Framework for Rural Enterprise Development Policy and Practice*, Bourton-on-Dunsmore: Practical Action, http://practicalaction.org/docs/ia2/mapping_the_market.pdf

Balsevich, F., Berdegue, J. A., Flores, L., Mainville, D., and Reardon, T. (2003) 'Supermarkets and produce quality and safety standards in Latin America', *American Journal of Agricultural Economics* 85 (5): 1147–54.

Batt, P. J. (2004) 'Cooperatives in Asia: when does intervention become an option?', in R. Trevin (ed.), *Cooperatives: Issues and Trends in Developing Countries*, ACIAR Technical Report No.53.

Biénabe, E. and Sautier, D. (2005) 'The Role of Small Scale Producers' Organisations to Address Markets Access', paper presented at Crop Post-Harvest workshop 'Beyond Agriculture: making markets work for the poor', 28 February and 1 March 2005, London: Crop Post Harvest Programme.

Bingen, J., Serrano, A., and Howard, J. (2003) 'Linking farmers to markets: different approaches to human capital development', *Food Policy* 28: 405–19.

Boselie, D. and van de Kop, P. (2005) 'Institutional and Organisational Change in Agri-Food Systems in Developing and Transitional Countries: Identifying Opportunities for Smallholders', Regoverning Markets global issue paper 2, Amsterdam: Royal Tropical Institute, www.kit.nl/smartsite.shtml?ch=fab&id=SINGLEPUBLICATION&ItemID=1927

Braverman, A., Guasch, J. L., Huppi, M., and Pohlmeier, L. (1991) 'Promoting Rural Cooperatives in Developing Countries: The Case of Sub-Saharan Africa', World Bank Discussion Papers, 121, Washington DC: The World Bank.

Cammack, J. (2002) *Basic Accounting for Small Groups (Second Revised Edition)*, Oxfam Skills & Practice Series, Oxford: Oxfam Publishing.

Cammack, J. (2007) *Building Capacity Through Financial Management: A Practical Guide*, Oxfam Skills & Practice Series, Oxford: Oxfam Publishing

Chirwa, E., Dorward, A., Kachule, R., Kumwenda, I., Kydd, J., Poole, N., Poulton, C., and Stockbridge, M. (2005) 'Farmer Organisations for Market Access: Principles for Policy and Practice', Department of Agricultural Sciences, Imperial College, London.

CLUSA (no date) 'Summary of Lessons Learnt and Best Practices for Developing Sustainable African Producer Organisations', Co-operative League of the USA.

Cook, M. L. and Iliopoulos, C. (1999) 'Beginning to inform the theory of the cooperative firm: emergence of the new generation cooperative', *The Finnish Journal of Business Economics* 4: 525–35.

Coulter, J., Goodland, A., Tallontire, A., and Stringfellow, R. (1999) 'Marrying Farmer Cooperation and Contract Farming for Service Provision in a Liberalising Sub-Saharan Africa', ODI Natural Resource Perspectives, no. 48, London: Overseas Development Institute.

Devereux, S. (2000) 'Food Insecurity in Ethiopia', a discussion paper for DFID, Brighton: Institute of Development Studies.

DFID (2004) 'Concentration in Food Supply and Retail Chains', Department for International Development, http://dfid-agriculture-consultation.nri.org/summaries/wp13.pdf

DFID (2005) 'Growth and Poverty Reduction: the Role of Agriculture', London: Department for International Development (DFID).

Diao, X., Dorosh, P., and Mahfuzur Rahman, S. (2003) 'Market Opportunities for African Agriculture: An Examination of Demand-Side Constraints on Agricultural Growth', Washington DC: International Food Policy Research Institute.

Dorward, A., Kydd, J., and Poulton, C. (1998) *Smallholder Cash Crop Production under Market Liberalisation, A New Institutional Economics Perspective*, Wallingford: CAB International.

Dorward, A., Kydd, J., Morrison, J., and Urey, I. (2004a) 'A policy agenda for pro-poor agricultural growth', *World Development* 32 (1): 73–89.

Dorward, A., Fan, S., Kydd, J., Lofgren, H., Morrison, J., Poulton, C., Rao, N., Smith, L., Tchale, H., Thorat, S., Urey, I., and Wobst, P. (2004b) 'Institutions and policies for pro-poor agriculture growth', *Development Policy Review* 22 (60): 611–22.

Ellman, A., Southgate, A., and Williams, P. (2004) 'Linking Farmers to Markets: A Manual for Helping Smallholder Farmers Access Markets by Working with Commercial Companies', (internal document), Oxford: Oxfam GB.

FAO (2004) *Helping Small Farmers Think About Better Growing and Marketing: A Reference Manual*, Rome: Food and Agricultural Organisation.

FAO (2005) *The State of Food and Agricultural*, FAO Agricultural Series, no. 36, Rome: Food and Agricultural Organisation.

Frederick, D. A. (1997) 'Co-ops 101: An Introduction to Cooperatives', Cooperative Information Report 55, Rural Business-Cooperative Service, U.S. Department of Agriculture, Washington D.C.

Giovannucci, D. and Satin, M. (no date) 'Food Quality Issues: Understanding HACCP and Other Quality Management Techniques', Washington DC: The World Bank, http://web.worldbank.org/WBSITE/EXTERNAL/TOPICS/EXTARD/0,,contentMDK:20440953~pagePK:210058~piPK:210062~theSitePK:336682,00.html

Giovannucci, D. and Reardon, T. (no date) 'Understanding Grades and Standards and How to Apply Them', Washington DC: The World Bank, http://web.worldbank.org/WBSITE/EXTERNAL/TOPICS/EXTARD/0,,contentMDK:20441034~pagePK:210058~piPK:210062~theSitePK:336682,00.html

Harper, M. (1992) *Their Own Idea, Lessons from Workers' Cooperatives*, London: ITDG Publishing.

Harper, M. and Roy, A. K. (2000) *Co-operative Success: What Makes Group Enterprises Succeed*, London: ITDG Publishing.

Hellin, J. and Higman, S. (2002) 'Smallholders and Niche Markets: Lessons from the Andes', AgRen Network Paper No.118, London: Overseas Development Institute.

Helvetas (2004) 'Clients First! A Rapid Market Appraisal (RMA) Tool Kit, Experience and Learning in International Cooperation', Helvetas Best Practice Publication, no. 3, Zurich: Helvetas, www.helvetas.ch/global/pdf/english/Professional_competences/Documented_experiences/resources/Clients_First_lowres.pdf

Hendrikse, G. and Veerman, C. (2001) 'Marketing cooperatives and financial structure: a transaction costs economics analysis', *Agricultural Economics* 26: 205–16.

Henehan, B. M. and Anderson, B. L. (2001) 'Considering Cooperation: a guide for new cooperative development', Department of Applied Economics and Management, College of Agriculture and Life Sciences, Cornell University, New York.

Heney, J. (2000) 'Enhancing farmers' financial management skills', *Agricultural Finance Revisited* (AFR), Rome: Food and Agriculture Organisation, www.ruralfinance.org/servlet/BinaryDownloaderServlet/2689_Document.pdf?filename=1128089435280_Enhancing_farmers_financial_management_skills.pdf&refID=2689

Hughes, D. (1994) 'Agroindustrial investment and operations: identifying, developing and servicing markets, in Brown, J. (ed.), *Agroindustrial Investment and Operations*, Washington DC: World Bank.

Humphrey, J. (2005) *Shaping Value Chains for Development: Global Value Chains for Agribusiness*, Eschborn: Deutsche Gesellschaft für Technische Zusammenarbeit (GTZ).

Humphrey, J. and Oetero, A. (2000) 'Strategies for Diversification and Adding Value to Food Exports: A Value Chain Perspective', United National Conference on Trade and Development, Geneva.

IAC (2004) 'The Role of Producer Organisations in Creating Market Access', final report, Wageningen: IAC Wageningen, http://portals.wi.wur.nl/files/docs/action/PO_Paper_Final_Report.pdf

IFAD (2001) *Rural Poverty Report 2001 – The Challenge of Ending Rural Poverty*, International Fund for Agricultural Development, Oxford: Oxford University Press.

ILO (2005) 'Legal Constraints to Women's Participation in Cooperatives: Country Studies from Burkina Faso, Cameroon, Ecuador, India, Lesotho, Morocco, the Philippines, Tanzania, Thailand and Uruguay', Cooperative Branch, Geneva: International Labour Office.

ILO (2005) 'Leadership Training Manuel for Women Leaders of Co-operatives', Geneva: International Labour Office, www.ica.coop/gender/publications.html

Jayne, T. S, Govereh, J., Mwanaumo, A., Chapoto, A., and Nyoro, J. K. (2001) 'False promise or false premise? The experience of food and input market reform in Eastern and Southern Africa', *World Development* 30 (11): 1967–85.

Jayne, T. S., Zulu, B., Mather, D., Mghenyi, E., Chirwa, E., and Tschirley, D. (2005) 'Maize Marketing and Trade Policy in a Pro-Poor Agricultural Growth Strategy: Insights from Household Surveys in Eastern and Southern Africa', paper prepared for the conference 'Towards Improved Maize Marketing and Trade Policies in the Southern Africa Region', sponsored by FANRPAN, 21–22 June 2005, South Africa: Centurion.

Kaplinsky, R. and Morris, M. (2003) 'A Handbook for Value Chain Research', Gapresearch.org, Brighton: IDS, www.ids.ac.uk/ids/global/pdfs/vchnov01.pdf

KIT, Faida MaLi, and IIRR (2006) *Chain Empowerment: Supporting African Farmers to Develop Markets*, Royal Tropical Institute (KIT), Faida MaLi, and International Institute of Rural Reconstruction (IIRR).

Koopmans, R. (2004) *Farmer-Controlled Economic Initiatives: Starting a Cooperative*, Wageningen: Agromisa Foundation.

Knight, S., Lyne, M., and Roth, M. (2003) 'Best Institutional Arrangements for Farmworker Equity-Share Schemes in South Africa', Department of Agricultural and Applied Economics, University of Wisconsin-Madison.

Kydd, J. and Dorward, A. (2004) 'Implication of market and coordination failures for rural development in least developed countries', *Journal of Development Studies* 16: 951–70.

Leys, C. (1996) *The Rise and Fall of Development Theory*, Oxford: James Currey.

Liu, P., Andersen, M., and Pazderka, C. (2004) 'Voluntary Standards and Certification for Environmentally and Socially Responsible Agricultural Production and Trade', Commodities and Trade Division, Rome: Food and Agricultural Organisation.

Lockwood, M. (2005) *The State They're In: An Agenda for International Development on Poverty in Africa*, Bourton-on-Dunsmore: ITDG Publishing.

Lundy, M., Gottret, M.V., Cifuentes, W., Ostertag, C.F., Best, R., Peters, D., and Ferris, S. (2004) *Increasing the Competitiveness of Market Chains for Smallholder Producers, Manual 3: Territorial Approach to Rural Agro-enterprise Development*, Columbia: International Centre for Tropical Agriculture.

Lundy, M., Ostertag, C. F., Gottret, M. V., Best, R., and Ferris, S. (2005a) 'A Territorial Approach to Rural Agro-enterprise Development: Strategy Paper: Territorial Approach to Rural Agro-enterprise Development', Columbia: International Centre for Tropical Agriculture.

Lundy, M., Gottret, M. V., Best, R., and Ferris, S. (2005b) *A Guide to Developing Partnerships, Territorial Analysis and Planning Together, Manual 1: Territorial Approach to Rural Agro-enterprise Development*, Columbia: International Centre for Tropical Agriculture.

Lutz. H. G. (2006) *Finding the Money: Farmer Organisation's Guide to Marketing for Small-Scale Farmers in Southern Africa*, Harare: Swedish Cooperative Centre.

Majluf, L. (2004) *Swimming in the Spaghetti Bowl: Challenges for Developing Countries Under the 'New Regionalism'*, Policy Issues in International Trade and Commodities, Study Series, no. 27, United Nations Conference on Trade and Development, Geneva.

Namken, J. C. and Rapp, G. W. (1997) *Strategic Planning Handbook for Cooperatives*, Cooperative Information Report 48, Rural Business-Cooperative Service, United States Department of Agriculture, Washington DC.

NRI (2003) *Small Producers in Export Horticulture – A Guide to Best Practice*, Chatham: Natural Resources Institute, www.nri.org/NRET/SPCDR/index.htm

Nussbaum, M. and Miehlbrandt, A. (2005) *How to Use Market Assessment Information to Design and Implement a BDS Market Development Program*, Discussion Synthesis No. 3, Washington DC: The Small Enterprise Education and Promotion (SEEP) Network, www.seepnetwork.org/content/library/detail/3140

Ostertag, C. F. (2004) *Identifying and Assessing Market Opportunities for Small-Scale Rural Producers, Manual 2: Territorial Approach to Rural Agro-enterprise Development*, Columbia: International Centre for Tropical Agriculture, www.ciat.cgiar.org/agroempresas/pdf/manual2_marketopportunity.pdf

Oxenham, J., Diallo, A. H., Ruhweza Katahoire, A., Petkova-Mwandi, A., and Sall, O. (2004) *Skills and Literacy Training for Better Livelihoods: A Review of Approaches and Experience*, Africa Region Human Development Working Paper Series, Washington DC: World Bank, http://www1.worldbank.org/education/adultoutreach/Doc/Skills%20and%20Literacy.pdf#search=%22Literacy%20and%20Numeracy%20CLUSA%22

Oxfam (2002) *Rigged Rules and Double Standards: Trade Globalisation and the Fight against Poverty*, Oxford: Oxfam Publishing.

Oxfam (2005) 'Best practice for farmer groups and cooperatives', presentation from Oxfam Livelihood Workshop, Havarana.

Ponte, S. (2001) 'The 'Latte Revolution'? Winners and Losers in the Restructuring of the Global Coffee Marketing Chain', CDR Working Paper 01.3, Copenhagen: Centre for Development Research.

Prinz, M. (2002) 'German Rural Cooperatives, Friedrich-Wilhelm Raiffeisen and the Organization of Trust, 1850 – 1914', paper delivered to XIII IEHA Congress, Buenos Aires.

Reardon, T., Codron, J., Busch, L., Bingen, J., and Harris, C. (2001) 'Global change in agrifood grades and standards: agribusiness strategic responses to developing countries', *International Food and Agribusiness Management Review* 2 (3/4): 421–35.

Reardon, T., Timmer, C., Barrett, C., and Berdegué, J. (2003) 'The rise of supermarkets in Africa, Asia and Latin America', *American Journal of Agricultural Economics*, Principal Paper Sessions, 85 (5): 1140–6.

Reardon, T. and Timmer, C. P. (2005) 'Transformation of markets for agricultural output in developing countries since 1950: how has thinking changed?', in R. E. Evenson, P. Pingali, and T. P. Schultz (eds.) *Handbook of Agricultural Economics, Volume 3: Agricultural Development: Farmer, Farm Production and Farm Markets*, Oxford: Elsevier Press.

Ritson, C. (1997) 'Marketing, agriculture and economics: presidential address', *Journal of Agricultural Economics* 48 (3): 279–99.

Robbins, P., Bikande, F., Ferris, S., Hodges, R., Kleih, U., Okoboi, G., and Wandschneider, T. (2004) *Advice Manual for the Organisation of Collective Marketing Activities for Small-scale Farmers*, Chatham: Natural Resources Institute, www.ciat.cgiar.org/agroempresas/pdf/manual4_collective marketing.pdf

Rosegrant, M. W., Ringler, C., Benson, T., Diao, X., Resnick, D., Thurlow, J., Torero, M., and Orden, D. (2006) *Agriculture and Achieving The Millennium Development Goals*, Washington DC: World Bank.

Roth, M. and Lyne, M. (2003) 'Institutional Innovations to Improve the Viability of Equity Sharing: Review of the Literature and Conceptual Framework for BASIS CRSP Research', Department of Agricultural and Applied Economics, University of Wisconsin-Madison.

Smyth, I., March, C., and Mukhopadhyay, M. (1998) *A Guide to Gender-analysis Frameworks*, Oxfam Skills & Practice Series, Oxford: Oxfam Publishing.

Stringfellow, R., Coulter, J., Lucey, T., McKone, C., and Hussain, A. (1997) 'Improving the Access of Smallholders to Agricultural Services in Sub-Saharan Africa: Farmer Cooperation and the Role of the Donor Community', *Natural Resources Perspectives* 20, London: Overseas Development Institute.

Suppan, S. (2001) 'Food Sovereignty in the Era of Trade Liberalisation: Are Multilateral Means Feasible?', Geneva: IATP, Geneva, www.fao.org/Regional/Lamerica/ong/cuba/pdf/02ofieng.pdf

Todaro, M. P. (1992) *Economics for a Developing World: An Introduction to Principles, Problems and Policies for Development*, third edition, New York: Longman.

Todaro, M. P. (2000) *Economic Development*, seventh edition, Boston: Addison-Wesley.

Traidcraft (no date) 'How to Find Market Information', Traidcraft, www.traidcraft.co.uk

Traidcraft (no date) 'Making the Most of Trade Fair Participation – a Toolkit', produced in collaboration with International Fund for Agricultural Development (IFAD), Traidcraft, www.traidcraft.co.uk

Traidcraft (2004) 'Into the Market Manual', produced in collaboration with International Fund for Agricultural Development (IFAD), Traidcraft, www.traidcraft.co.uk

UCDA (2006) 'UCDA Monthly Report for July 2006', Uganda Coffee Development Authority.

van Dooren, P. J. (1982). *Co-operatives for Developing Countries: Objectives, Policies and Practices*, Oxford: Parchment Limited.

van Roekel, J., Kopicki, R., Broekmans, C., and Boselie, D. (2002). *Building Agri Supply Chains: Issues and Guidelines*, Washington DC: World Bank.

Vermeulen, S. (2005) *Power Tools: Handbook to Tools and Resources for Policy Influence in Natural Resource Management*, London: International Institute for Environment & Development.

Vorley, B. (2001) 'The Chains of Agriculture: Sustainability and Restructuring of Agri-food Markets', IIED's opinion in preparation for World Summit on Sustainable Development, International Institute for Environment and Development.

Vorley, B. and Fox, T. (2004) 'Global Food Chains – Constraints and Opportunities for Smallholders', IIED, prepared for the OECD DAC POVNET, Agriculture and Pro-Poor Growth Task Team, Helsinki Workshop, www.oecd.org/dataoecd/24/60/36562581.pdf

Watkins, K. and von Braun, J. (2003) 'Time to Stop Dumping on the World's Poor', IFPRI Annual Report 2002–03, Washington DC: International Food Policy Research Institute.

Weatherspoon, D. and Reardon, T. (2003) 'The rise of supermarkets in Africa: the implications for agrifood systems and the rural poor', *Development Policy Review* 21 (3): 333–55.

Weinstein, K. (2002) *Action Learning, A Practical Guide*, Aldershot: Gower Publishing Company.

Williams, S., Seed, J., and Mwau, A. (1995) *The Oxfam Gender Training Manual*, Oxford: Oxfam Publishing.

World Bank (1981) *Accelerated Development in Sub-Saharan Africa: An Agenda for Action*, Washington DC: World Bank.

World Bank (1994) *Adjustment in Africa: Reforms, Results and the Road Ahead*, New York: Oxford University Press.

World Bank (2003) *Reaching the Rural Poor: A Renewed Strategy for Rural Development*, Washington DC: The World Bank.

World Bank (2005) *Agricultural Growth for the Poor: An Agenda for Development*, Washington DC: The World Bank.

Index

ACDI/VOCA 43, 65
activities of producer organisations (POs)
    2–4, 32–3, 34, 70, 117–18, 129–34
    see also services provided
Africa 70 see also specific countries and
    regions
Agrolempa, El Salvador
    activities and services 32–3, 34, 44
    benefits of POs 20, 25, 29, 44
    business strategies 55, 59, 62, 111, 118
    financial issues 51
    governance and management 48, 49
    market services access 65
    structure 39, 40, 44, 73, 122
Albania 19, 20, 24, 27, 103 see also
    Zadrima Co-operative
Alternative Trading Organisations (ATOs)
    ix, x, 80
Aprainores (Agro-Industrial Association
    of Organic Producers of El Salvador) 94,
    109, 124, 129
AProCA (Association of Cotton Producers
    of Africa) 70, 71, 85, 132, 133
Asia 7 see also East Asia; South-East Asia
Asprepatía (Association of Panela
    Producers of the Patía Region),
    Colombia 20, 35, 60, 65, 69–70, 115,
    118, 133

benefits of producer organisations (POs)
    18, 19–23, 25, 26
    access improved viii, xi–xiii, 20, 21, 22
    bargaining power 18, 20–3, 25, 59–61,
    118
    benefits to wider community 28–9
    confidence building 3, 5, 23, 28, 70
    economies of scale 19–20, 21, 22, 53, 58
    influence increased viii, xii, 18, 23
    lower costs 19, 20, 22
    value adding opportunities 22, 55–7
    for women 20, 23, 28
business strategies of producer
    organisations (POs)
    adding value 55–7, 73, 162
    bargaining power 55, 59–61, 125, 162
    brand creation 55–6, 73, 131–2, 135
    business planning 113–14, 152–3
    certification 56, 121, 163
    cost reduction 58–9, 75, 118, 121
    diversification 56, 58, 62, 75
    increasing income 55–8, 75
    market development 58, 75, 89–90,
    110–13
    market research strategies 100,
    109–13, 151
    market risk reduction 62–3, 111
    processing as a strategy 56–7, 59,
    129–31, 135

178

CAN (Centros de Apoio e de Negócios) 65–6
capacity building in producer organisations (POs)
  capacity appraisal 93–4, 97–8, 103, 148–55
  grassroots capacity 50–1, 52, 84, 101–4, 149
  management capacity 61, 113–17, 149–50
  marketing capacity 64, 75, 81, 91, 151–2, 154–5
  membership capacity 50–1, 52, 90
  production capacity 90, 94, 112, 119, 125, 131–2, 153–4
  structure relationship 43, 45, 50, 52, 74, 76
  support organisations involvement ix–x, 43, 80
    facilitating agencies 86, 91, 97–8, 100, 101–4, 113–17, 125
    NGOs x, 61, 75–6, 78, 81, 82, 84
  for women 50, 102, 103–4, 125
cashew nut production 94, 124
Central Africa 70, 85
Central America 51
Clam Clubs, Viet Nam
  business strategies 62, 118, 125
  financial issues 51–2, 115–16
  NGO support 38, 84, 116, 125, 127, 134
  structure 38–9, 43, 89
CLUSA (Co-operative League of the USA) 46, 51, 65, 66, 70–1, 79, 80, 102
cocoa production 11, 58, 59, 106, 115, 131–2
coffee production 11, 13, 27, 35, 51, 53, 58, 107
Common Market for Eastern and Southern Africa (COMESA) 10
community-based organisations 2, 26, 39, 136, 138
competitiveness and producer organisations (POs) 3, 35, 38–9, 55, 89, 90, 110, 129–30
COMUCAP, Honduras 3, 23, 28, 35, 49, 83–4
cotton production 19, 22, 56, 59–61, 70, 82, 85, 129

developed countries 9, 10, 12, 14, 130, 163
developing countries 5, 7, 9–10, 11, 14–15, 65, 163
disadvantages of producer organisations (POs) xi–xiii, 26–8
Dominican Republic 103 *see also* Fedecares

East Asia 15
Eastern Africa 15
El Salvador 44 *see also* Agrolempa; Aprainores
Ethiopia 26, 29, 34

facilitating agencies (FAs) and producer organisations (POs)
  assessing minimum conditions 89–90
  business and social services provision 86, 93, 102–3, 108, 152–3
  co-ordinated approach 86, 88, 91, 94
  defined 164
  exit strategies 94–6, 98, 124–5
  and failing businesses 87, 92
  in formation of new POs 91–3, 136–8
  gender issues 93, 94, 98, 103–4, 107, 137
  independence promotion 86, 89, 90
  long-term approach 86, 88, 89
  and the market environment 87, 89–90
  poverty issues 93–4, 98
  rapid market and producer assessment 90–1, 98, 144–7
  realistic expectations 87, 93–4
  support strategies
    advocacy work 132–4, 135
    assessing and implementing support 96–8, 99
    brand creation 131–2, 135
    capacity building 86, 91, 97–8, 100, 101–4, 113–17, 125
    confidence-building strategies 102
    financial support 114–17, 122–3, 134, 137–8
    gender issues 98, 103–4, 107, 122, 125
    governance and leadership issues 104–9
    market research and marketing strategies 109–13, 151–2

Index | 179

market services access 126–8
ownership and control issues 101,
  101–3, 104, 160
processing strategies 129–31, 135
production strategies 117–21
skills improvement strategies 102,
  103, 104, 125
social-capital building 106–7, 108,
  123, 161
structure support 121–3
support principles 86–7
tools *see* tools for support below
trade linkages 123–6
tools for support
  capacity appraisal 93–4, 97–8, 103,
    148–55
  formation of new POs 160–1
  legal structure overview 156–9
  rapid assessment of markets and
    producers 144–7
Fairtrade Labelling Organisation 16, 120
Fairtrade products 12–13, 16, 112, 120
Fedecares, Dominican Republic 50–1, 85,
  105
financial issues of producer organisations
  (POs) 19, 27, 33–4
  business cost management 114–15
  distribution of profits 37, 39, 40, 41,
    47, 51–2, 157
  financial risks 24–5, 62–3, 89, 92, 93,
    111, 129–30, 157
  financial support 69, 83–4, 89, 92–3,
    114–17, 122–3, 134, 137–8
  investment issues 38, 40, 41, 51–2,
    115–17, 130, 131–2, 158
  sustainability issues 35, 47, 83–4, 86,
    95, 98, 122–3, 164
  taxation 38, 39, 42, 158
  see also transaction costs
FLO-Cert 120
forming new producer organisations
  (POs) 91–3, 136–8, 160–1
fruit and vegetable production 10, 14, 20,
  29, 34, 44, 59, 123

gender issues 93, 94, 98, 103–4, 107
  see also women
GEPA, Germany 80
Ghana 8, 66 *see also* Kuapa Kokoo
government agencies ix, 65, 79–80, 84,
  91, 110, 118, 146
grades and standards (G&S) 15–16, 165
groundnut production 34, 55, 120
Gumatindu, Uganda 53
Guyana Rice Producers' Association 23

Hazard Analysis Critical Control Points
  (HACCP) 16

India 19, 81, 82
Indonesia 89
industrialised countries *see* developed
  countries
International Co-operative Alliance (ICA)
  40
International Commodity Agreements 11,
  165

Kenya 25
Kiwi Growers' Co-operative, Georgia 92–3
Kuapa Kokoo, Ghana 59, 106, 115, 131–2

land issues and producer organisations
  (POs) 32, 46, 67, 90, 112
Latin America 9, 15

maize production 8, 10, 47, 53–4, 56, 60
Malawi 40, 89, 105, 112, 120 *see also*
  NASFAM
MAPRONET, Ghana 66, 134
the market
  buyer-driven markets 21, 62, 67, 84
  global trends viii, 5, 10–13, 17
  market access issues viii, xii–xiii, 5, 8,
    20, 21, 46–7, 67, 119
  market chains 7, 13–15, 21, 166
  market concentration 13–14, 166
  market liberalisation viii, 5, 7–8, 17,
    67, 166
  market linkages 62–3, 154–5, 166
  market services 64–6, 81, 84, 114,
    126–8, 166

180 | *Producer Organisations: A Guide to Developing Collective Rural Enterprises*

'thin' markets 8–10, 19, 28, 168
value chains 13, 14–15, 169
market environment and producer organisations (POs) 67–71, 87, 89–90
market services access and producer organisations (POs) 64–6, 75, 81, 84, 114, 126–8, 166
Mozambique
  co-operatives 41
  maize production 56
  market environment 67, 70
  NGO support 51, 53–4, 65, 80, 82–3, 123, 124, 130
  see also UCASN

NASFAM (National Smallholder Farmers' Association of Malawi)
  activities and services 34, 44, 70
  benefits of POs 23, 24, 70, 90
  brand creation 131
  business strategies 55, 58, 112, 118, 131
  communication methods 106
  financial issues 89, 115
  governance and management 48, 50
  market services access 65
  quality management issues 34, 55, 120
  structure 39–40, 43, 44, 105, 108
networks of producer organisations (POs) 66, 71, 81, 132, 134
New Generation Co-operative (NGC) 41
NGO support for producer organisations (POs) ix–xi, 79, 80–1
  business and social services provision 35, 83–4, 86, 93
  facilitating approach 81, 82–3, 84–5 see also facilitating agencies
  financial support 9, 83–4, 89, 92–3
  hands-on approach 82–3
  in market environment 70
  market services provision 65, 66, 81, 84
  strategic role 84–6
  strengths and weaknesses 80–1, 82, 83
  see also CLUSA; facilitating agencies; Oxfam GB
North America Free Trade Agreement (NAFTA) 10

OAPI (Oorvi Agricultural Products India) 56, 59–61, 82, 120, 129
OCDIH (Organismo Cristiano de Desarrollo Integral de Honduras) 132–3
olive-oil co-operatives, Palestine 22, 40, 54–5, 70, 89
organic products 12, 61, 112
Oxfam GB
  and Aprainores 94, 124
  and Asprepatía 69
  business strategy involvement 54, 57, 58, 60–1, 102–3
  and Clam Clubs 38, 84, 115–16, 125, 127, 134
  and OAPI 60–1, 82
  support for producer organisations (POs)
    advocacy work 81, 85, 134
    assessments 89, 90, 93
    assistance with management 46, 47
    capacity building 61, 90, 125
    exit strategies 94
    financial support 38, 49, 57, 69, 89, 92, 115–16
    market linkages 124, 125
    market services provision 66, 81, 127
    skills training 38
    strengths and weaknesses 80–1
    support approaches 82, 84, 85
    for women 85, 103
    and UCASN 46, 47, 80–1, 85, 102–3
    and Zadrima 90, 127

Palestinian Farmers Union (PFU) 54
Palestinian Olive Oil Council 54–5
panela production 34, 61, 62, 69–70
poverty reduction and producer organisations (POs) 61, 83, 93–4, 98
private companies and producer organisations (POs) 3, 41–2, 44, 48, 61, 80, 118, 157–9
processing and producer organisations (POs) 15, 56–7, 61, 73, 129–31, 135, 168
producer organisations (POs) defined viii–ix, 2–4

production and producer organisations
  (POs)
  cash-crop production 11, 72
  collective production 3, 118, 146
  high-value food production 12–13, 27,
    56, 58, 72, 112, 165
  improving production
    certification schemes 16–17, 56, 67,
      120–1
    co-ordinating output 117–18, 121
    diversification 11, 56, 58, 62, 164
    food-safety issues 14, 15, 16, 34, 55,
      112, 119, 120, 165
    increasing output 118, 121
    new product standards 15–16
    production services 33, 34
    quality management 14, 15, 34,
      55–6, 112, 119–20, 121, 131
    traceability 14, 15
  production capacity 90, 94, 112, 119,
    125, 131–2, 153–4
  staple food production 10–11, 27
  see also specific crops

regional trade agreements (RTAs) 10
risks and costs of producer organisations
  (POs) 19, 23–5, 27, 45
  financial risks 24–5, 62–3, 89, 92, 93,
    111, 129–30, 157
  free riding 24–5
  governance problems 24, 45, 47, 107, 108
  transaction cost increases 24, 59
  trust issues 24, 42, 45, 50, 74, 90, 101,
    107
  see also disadvantages of producer
    organisations
rural businesses as producer
  organisations (POs) 2–3, 4, 26, 67, 83

services provided by producer
  organisations (POs) 32–3, 36, 67
  advocacy work 43, 69, 70–1, 73, 85,
    132–4, 135, 155, 169
  business services 33–5, 36, 83–4, 125, 155
  lobbying role 44, 69, 70, 85, 112,
    132–3, 134
  social services 2–3, 29, 35, 83–4

small-scale producers
  better-off producers xiii, 26, 27
  cash-crop production 11, 72
  commercial priorities viii, 2–3
  competitiveness xii, 3, 90, 110
  contract farming schemes 16–17
  defined xiii–xiv
  high-value food production 12–13, 27,
    56, 58, 72, 112
  land issues 26, 46, 67, 90, 112
  and the market
    buyer-driven markets 21, 62, 67, 84
    economies of scale 19–20, 21, 22, 58
    global market trends viii, 5, 10–13, 17
    market access issues xii–xiii, 5, 8,
      20, 21, 67
    market chains 13–14, 21
    market liberalisation viii, 5, 8, 17, 67
    market services 64–6, 81, 84, 114,
      126
    supermarket relationships 15, 19
    'thin' markets 8–10, 19, 28
    in a market environment 67–71, 87,
      89–90
  NGO relationships 9, 28, 79, 81, 90–1,
    94, 96, 112
  poor producers xiii, 26–7, 28, 112
  and producer organisations (POs)
    benefits of viii, xii–xiii, 19–23, 25,
      26, 28, 33
    collective marketing activities 3,
      26, 34, 70
    disadvantages ix, xi–xiii, 26–8,
      41–2, 52
    ownership and control issues 3, 41,
      47, 49–51, 52
    risks and costs 19, 23–5, 27, 28, 45,
      62–3, 92, 93
    staple food production 10–11, 27
    transaction costs 19, 20, 22, 24, 27,
      53–4, 58–9
SNV (Netherlands Development
  Organisation) 79
social capital in producer organisations
  (POs) 24, 90, 106–7, 108, 123, 161, 168
South Africa 15
South-East Asia 15

Southern Africa 15, 53, 83
St Lucia 56, 58, 85, 124
structure of producer organisations (POs)
  associations 39–40, 42, 43, 44, 46–7, 157–9
  capacity-building relationship 43, 45, 50, 52, 74, 76
  co-operatives 34, 39–40, 41, 42, 51, 54–5, 56–7, 157–9
  development of POs 72–6, 90, 122–3
  and facilitating agencies 121–3, 156–9
  governance 47–8, 49, 50, 52
    governance vs. management 44
  NGO support 104–9
  problems 24, 45, 47, 107, 108
  and social capital 24, 90, 106–7, 108
  trust issues 24, 42, 45, 50, 74, 90, 101, 107
  hybrid structures 41
  informal organisations 39, 73
  legal structure 37–42, 89, 104–6, 121–2, 123, 156–9
  management 44, 46, 47, 48–9, 74, 113–17, 123
  membership issues 37, 41, 50–1, 118, 157
  multi-level and mixed structures 41, 42–5, 47, 50, 54–5, 73, 122–3
  ownership and control issues
    for new POs 160
    NGO support 101, 102–3, 104, 160
    overview 157
    small-scale producers 3, 41, 47, 49–51, 52
    private company involvement 3, 41–2, 44, 48, 61, 157–9
    for processing 130
    size issues 42, 73, 132, 137
    voting rights 37, 40, 41, 47, 101, 105, 157
sub-Saharan Africa 7, 11, 25, 89–90, 102
supermarkets 13, 14–15, 19, 120
support for producer organisations (POs)
  donors ix–x, 49, 65, 71, 80, 85, 122
  facilitating agencies (FAs) see under facilitating agencies

financial support 69, 83–4, 89, 92–3, 114–17, 122–3, 134, 137–8
government agencies ix–x, 64, 65, 79–80, 84, 91, 110, 118, 146
NGOs see under NGO support
private companies ix–x, 80, 118
structure support 121–3, 156–9
support approaches 82–4

tobacco production 23, 43, 70
trade and producer organisations (POs)
  informal trading 25, 33, 39, 47, 52–3, 61
  in 'thin' markets 8–10, 19, 20–1
  trade liberalisation 7, 9–10, 84
  trade linkages 123–6, 154–5
  trading companies 32–3, 34, 44
training 33, 34, 38, 50–1, 65, 102–4, 118, 135
transaction costs
  defined 8–9, 169
  and economies of scale 19, 20, 22, 53, 58
  for small-scale producers 19, 20, 22, 24, 27, 53–4, 58–9
  in 'thin' markets 8–9, 19
Twin Trading, UK 80

UCASN (Union of Peasants and Associations of Southern Niassa), Mozambique
  benefits of POs 22
  business strategies 56, 58, 60, 62, 102–3
  financial issues 51, 52
  governance and management 46–7, 48, 50
  market services access 65
  NGO support 70–1, 80–1, 85, 102–3
  structure 45, 122
UFP (Union of Fruit Producers), West Africa 49, 50, 105, 107, 122
Uganda 13, 27, 53, 107
United States Agency for International Development (USAID) 80

vegetable production *see* fruit and
    vegetable production
Viet Nam 39, 85 *see also* Clam Clubs

West Africa 22, 49, 85, 132
wine production 19, 20, 24, 27, 56–7,
    73–4, 90, 129
women
    market access issues 8, 67
    NGO support 85, 103–4
    and producer organisations (POs)
        benefits 20, 23, 28
        capacity-building opportunities 50,
            102, 103–4, 125
        membership issues 50–1, 74, 93,
            103–4, 105, 107, 122, 137
        skills improvement 50–1, 102–4, 125
        social service provision 23, 35
        and social capital 107

Zadrima Co-operative, Albania 56–7,
    73–4, 90, 129, 131